WORDS AND DEEDS

Birmingham Suffragists and Suffragettes
1832-1918

Nicola Gauld

Published by West Midlands History Limited

Minerva Mill Innovation Centre, Alcester, Warwickshire, UK.

© 2018 West Midlands History Limited.

© All images are copyright as credited.

ISBN: 978-1-905036-43-1

Cover image: PUNCH Magazine Cartoon Archive.

Caric Press Limited, Merthyr Tydfil, Wales.

This book is dedicated to Eliza, Catherine, Hilda, Maude, Bertha and all the other Birmingham women who fought for our right to vote.

Acknowledgements

I am grateful to Malcolm Dick for suggesting that Mike Gibbs approach me as a potential person to tell this story and I would like to thank Mike for being so enthusiastic and supportive throughout. I would especially like to thank my editor, Jenni Butterworth, without whom this book would not have been possible; Jenni's keen eye, enthusiasm and encouragement have made writing the book an extremely enjoyable experience. I would like to thank Sean Griffiths and Helen Cross for their work on the accompanying documentary. The helpfulness of the archivists at the Library of Birmingham, Cadbury Research Library (especially Helen Fisher), Sarah Foden and Sarah Welch from Mondelez International, Alison Wheatley from King Edward's Schools and the Women's Library at the LSE was invaluable. Thanks also to Maggie Andrews for her helpful comments and suggestions. I would also like to thank my colleagues at Women's History Birmingham, Brigitte Winsor, Nikki Thorpe and Sian Roberts, for their solidarity and support. Nikki was especially instrumental in my research into the Birmingham suffrage campaign, supporting my work on the Fight for the Right: the Birmingham Suffragettes project in 2012, and the research that came afterwards. I would like to thank Ian Grosvenor for his continued support and friendship. Finally, I wish to thank my parents, Hilda and Gordon, my brother Stephen and his partner Mhairi, and my beautiful niece Tabitha. I could not have written it without their love, support and encouragement.

Contents

1 Introduction

5 Chapter one
Votes for women: the early campaign; 1832 – 1906

21 Chapter two
The beginnings of militancy in the city: 1906 – 1909

51 Chapter three
Campaigning, census evasion and increased militancy:
1910 – 1912

66 Chapter four
The peak of militant tactics: 1913 – 1914

93 Chapter five
War and its aftermath: 1914 – 1918

108 Afterword

110 Notes

117 Index

Introduction

On 17 September 1909 Liberal Prime Minister Herbert Asquith, a staunch anti-suffragist, visited Bingley Hall, in the centre of Birmingham (the site is now occupied by the International Convention Centre on Broad Street). He was in the city to attend the Budget League Demonstration where he would discuss radical proposals put forward by the Chancellor of the Exchequer, David Lloyd George. Records show that the authorities were prepared for disruption by members of the Women's Social & Political Union (WSPU), or 'suffragettes' as they were now being called by the newspapers, and the police presence was significant. Instructions were given to the police that 'all tickets are marked not to admit a lady except certain special tickets' and to avoid using unnecessary violence but also that they should carefully scrutinise each person entering in case any women attempted to gain admission while dressed as men.[1]

Determined on disruption, however, two of the suffragettes, Mary Leigh and Charlotte Marsh, members from London sent up for the demonstration, climbed onto the roof of a timber merchant's premises in Cambridge Street and threw roof slates at Asquith's car. Outside the Hall six other women tried to break through the barriers and it was observed that repeated attempts to send the women away failed. As the Prime Minister went to leave for the train station events took a farcical turn: Marsh and Leigh were threatened with a fire hose, and although the pressure was said to have been insufficient for the stream of water to reach them, they were eventually dragged soaking wet from the roof and were reported to have cried, 'Do what you like. We want votes for members of Parliament. Do your worst', followed by 'Liberty or death!'[2] Altogether ten women were arrested in connection with the incident, which was widely reported in local and national newspapers. This included two women from Birmingham: Hilda Burkitt, a secretary living in Sparkbrook, and Ellen Barnwell, a clerk from Selly Oak, both accused of throwing objects at Asquith's train as it left the station. All ten were taken to the police station on Steelhouse Lane and then to Winson Green Gaol.

A meeting of 'suffragists', or members of the Birmingham Women's Suffrage Society (BWSS), advocates of constitutional and educational means of campaigning, was held that same evening at the Birmingham & Midland Institute. In her role as President of the Birmingham Women's Liberal Association, Catherine Osler, who was also President of the BWSS, had been permitted entry into the budget meeting at Bingley Hall. However, her frustration with the Government was made clear in a letter that she had sent to be read on her behalf at the suffrage meeting: reported in *The Common Cause*, the NUWSS newspaper, she observed that 'women citizens had undoubted reason to feel insulted and injured when denied the right of listening to the exposition by the Prime Minister of proposals which affected them equally with men, and on which they were refused the expression of an opinion through the vote. The injury and insult would be most keenly felt by those who like herself strongly condemned disorder and violence as a means of public agitation'. The fact that such examples of 'public agitation'[3] would attract the attention of newspaper editors was another source of frustration for her. Osler had been a tireless campaigner for women's suffrage since the BWSS was established by her parents in 1868, spending decades patiently lobbying Parliament, publishing articles and carrying out social and educational work.

The incident at Bingley Hall in September 1909 changed the direction of the campaign for women's votes, ushering in a new wave of militancy and leading to a dramatic development in the punishment the women received. It also encapsulates the division between the two different sides of the campaign for women's enfranchisement, one constitutional, the other militant. There had been suffrage societies active in Britain since the 1860s and the National Union of Women's Suffrage Societies, led by Millicent Garrett Fawcett, had been formed in the 1890s. Despite their dedication and hard work very little progress had been made and so, in 1903, the Women's Social & Political Union was established by Emmeline Pankhurst and her daughters Christabel and Sylvia at the family home in Manchester. In Birmingham, the WSPU and the BWSS, one of the earliest regional suffrage societies in the country, operated in tandem, sometimes working collaboratively (indeed, some women held membership of both groups), but were more frequently opposed in their methods during the long fight to secure women the right to vote. Both organisations essentially fought for the same outcome: parliamentary votes for women on the same terms as men, that is, determined by a property qualification. Of course, this did not apply to all men – only 58% were enfranchised at the beginning of the 20th century, prior to the passing of the Representation of the People Act of 1918.

Although achieving votes for women would represent a partial victory only, if and when it came, the argument presented by both sides was that progress needed to be gradual and that eventually all women would be given the right to vote. The priority for now was to begin the journey to equality by removing the sex barrier. Some were suspicious, however, of a campaign led by middle-class women which did not advocate universal suffrage – votes for all men and women aged over 21. Birmingham's role in the campaign is often overlooked in favour of activities that took place in London and

Manchester but the city was home to Catherine Osler, a friend and loyal supporter of Millicent Fawcett, and it saw some incredible acts of militancy. It also has the more unfortunate claim of being the site of the first instance of forcible feeding of hunger-striking suffragette prisoners, a consequence of the Bingley Hall demonstration.

In order to tell the story of the suffrage campaign in Birmingham this book will draw on newspapers of the period, both local and national, as well as the suffrage organisations' own publications, primarily the WSPU's *Votes for Women* and later on *The Suffragette*, and the NUWSS's *The Common Cause*, along with annual reports published by the BWSS over a 40-year period, archive material held in local and national collections, and the extensive work carried out by Elizabeth Crawford, whose pamphlet 'From Frederick Street to Winson Green: the women's suffrage movement in Birmingham 1866-1918' provided an essential starting point for my own research. Suffrage newspapers were a way for the organisations to provide a manifesto for the movement, to share information about campaign activities that were taking place across the country and also to tell the stories of their activities from their own perspective. In recognition of the power of the press, many WSPU actions were designed specifically in order to attract press attention and keep the cause on the front pages of the newspapers, thereby preventing politicians from ignoring the campaign at a time when Irish Home Rule and particularly the crisis of 1912 and the rise of the Ulster Volunteers, and the looming possibility of war with Germany, threatened to overshadow arguments around giving women the right to vote. *Votes for Women* was the most widely circulated over the five-year period of its publication and included in-depth articles that explained the tactics being employed, biographies of various personalities, and weekly updates on the activities of local WSPU branches. It is particularly invaluable as a source because there are so few surviving records of the WSPU. After a split within the WSPU leadership the Pankhursts began another journal, *The Suffragette*, published from 1912, although this did not have the same reach as *Votes for Women*. *The Common Cause* was first published in 1909, enabling local committees to keep in touch with wider NUWSS activities across the country. Local updates printed in all three journals reveal much about how the branches in Birmingham were run and by whom and about the types of activities that they were involved with.

Celebrating in 2018 the centenary of the Representation of the People Act that gave some women the vote and the 90th anniversary of the Equal Franchise Act which gave all men and women over the age of 21 the vote, it is important to examine, understand and recognise those campaigners who were active over 100 years ago – their methods, their actions and the unrelenting dedication to the cause over many decades.

The book will explore the campaign by both organisations (while there were other suffrage organisations, the BWSS and WSPU dominated in Birmingham) and will detail incidents that have largely been forgotten within the region. By considering the political activity in the city that led to the formation in 1868 of the BWSS it will become clear that Birmingham has always been a political city, capable of running campaigns that focus on civic and social improvement. The book will then explore how the campaign for women's votes developed during the 19th century and resulted in the establishment of a WSPU branch in the city in 1907. The peak of militant activity in the subsequent years, particularly 1913-1914 when incidents occurred on an almost weekly basis, will be examined, as will the often harrowing experiences of the women themselves, alongside public reaction to these incidents, ranging from sympathy and changed minds to downright violent hostility. Finally, the impact of the Great War on the campaign and the partial victory gained in 1918 when women over the age of 30 who met the property qualification were permitted to vote in general elections will be considered.

The book will explore infamous incidents carried out by the militant suffragettes, extreme acts such as the destruction of Northfield Library and vandalism at the city's Art Gallery, alongside the steadfast and unrelenting constitutional campaigning by the BWSS, led for over twenty years by Catherine Osler. Although each suffrage organisation had its own methods and preferred tactics, there were many complexities to this, and overlapping memberships and collaborative efforts between groups have often been forgotten at the expense of presenting a narrative of a campaign rife with division and animosity. The determination and dedication of women belonging to both groups, and their role in securing the right for women to vote – a right that must never be taken lightly – should be recognised within the city, their actions laying the path for politicians and activists here today. Catherine Osler and Hilda Burkitt may be names that have been forgotten by some but their contribution to women's rights 100 years ago must not be. This book is dedicated to Catherine, Hilda and all those other Birmingham women who fought for our right to vote.

Votes for Women: the early campaign in Birmingham: 1832-1906

'When words needed saying and deeds needed doing,
were women to sit down and talk about their "spheres"?'

Eliza Sturge

Meddling with politics

The issue of votes for women had been in the minds of some men and women for decades prior to the rise of the militant suffrage campaign of the early twentieth century. The first petition to Parliament on the subject of women's votes had been presented in 1832, however, the Great Reform Act of that year had defined voters as 'male persons', definitively excluding women. Following the Act, Birmingham had achieved Parliamentary status, becoming a borough in its own right, and returned Thomas Attwood, founder of the Birmingham Political Union (BPU), as the city's first member.[4] Calls for universal suffrage continued throughout the 1830s but while this did not include extending the franchise to women, women did participate in the many political discussions led by the Chartists, after the movement gained momentum in 1838 with publication of the People's Charter. In April of that year a meeting at the Town Hall of the Birmingham Political Union was reported on the front page of the radical newspaper *The Birmingham Journal*. A massive (and possibly over-exaggerated) attendance figure of 12,000 was later given in an article in *Votes for Women*, the first newspaper of the Women's Social & Political Union, which cited a letter written by Thomas Clutton Salt, one of the leaders of the BPU and a delegate of the first Chartist delegation. Here Salt had claimed 'there could not have been less than 12,000 women' present at the meeting, 'a more beautiful and moving sight was never seen, a meeting more enthusiastic or orderly was never assembled, it was evident that the iron had entered their souls, and that they felt deeply and resolved religiously that their children's children should not be trampled on as they had been'. Salt continued, 'now the women of Birmingham would obtain the immortal honour of setting an example to the women of England which would be of the utmost consequence to all'.[5]

A few months later, in August 1838, Salt held a meeting to establish a Female Political Union, although this was designed to support the push for men's suffrage, not to campaign for the vote for women.[6] A large crowd of around 750 people, significantly less than the April meeting, was present to hear Salt. He later wrote a letter to the women of Birmingham, urging them to 'meddle with politics'.[7] George Edmonds, another of the

Birmingham Chartists, was also present. Clearly supportive of women becoming more politically active and recognising the strengths women could bring to campaigning, Edmonds wrote: 'If the women of England took up the subject of politics – if they set about ascertaining the real causes of the misery of themselves and families and resolved upon removing them, there was no doubt they could do it. If the women would meet, and unite, and co-operate, with due discretion and determination, they would do more in one year than the men could by themselves in many years.'[8]

The women of Birmingham took Edmonds up on his challenge and at the end of August the first meeting of the Female Political Union was held: 1,300 tickets had been issued and a chairwoman had been appointed. Although women were enthusiastic participants, one of the women speakers described the hostile reaction she had received from Tory acquaintances, 'who demanded to know what right had she to busy herself about politics', an objection that some men would make repeatedly throughout the campaign to secure women the vote. The speaker responded that 'by leaving politics entirely to the men, her condition, and that of her neighbours, was getting worse'.[9] Women would have to fight for themselves if they were to improve their lives. Towards the end of September 'the Union had nearly 3,000 members and had raised 13,000 signatures for a women's petition for the Charter'.[10] Weekly meetings continued throughout 1838 but by March 1839 attendance had dropped dramatically and the Union's chairwoman, Mrs Lapworth, reported at the meeting on 18 March that 'if she had been rightly informed, there was some secret influence at work, to damage their union'.[11]

While opponents of the movement sought to undermine it, and held particular objections to the involvement of women, there were also divisions within the Chartist movement itself over the use of constitutional versus militant means, a debate that would also recur during the women's movement of the early 20th century, and 'at the end of March 1839, four of the six Birmingham delegates to the National Convention, including Salt, resigned over the continued use of physical-force language at the Convention. By the end of the following month, the BPU had been suspended'.[12] This was seen as a betrayal by some members of the Female Political Union, Lapworth included, and the women's group was left without a promoter or meeting place. Lapworth set the tone for women campaigners, stating at a meeting 'we have been obliged to practise the art of speaking for ourselves, for no man's mouth was open on our behalf'.[13] Despite attempts to damage the organisation, the Female Political Union continued to hold weekly meetings throughout 1839 and, although it had not been established with the aim of securing votes for women, it clearly gave women a platform from which they could assert their political opinions. The speed at which Birmingham women had mobilised, and the strength and skill they showed in pushing for reform alongside men, demonstrated that the female citizens of Birmingham could easily provide a stronghold for any reforming movement.

'The movement continues to acquire strength'

The 1860s saw the campaign for women's suffrage gain traction and intensify. In 1866 the first mass petition on the subject of women's suffrage was presented to Parliament by the MP John Stuart Mill with 1,521 signatures, marking the start of organised campaigning for women's votes. Names were collected at the London home of Clementia Taylor, who was married to the radical MP and suffragist Peter Alfred Taylor.[14] Only four of the names definitely belonged to Birmingham householders: Mrs Ash, Sarah Clark, Susannah Hood, and Elizabeth Train.[15] A women's suffrage committee was formed in London and in the following year Lydia Becker founded the Manchester National Society for Women's Suffrage. Despite women becoming more organised, the extension to the franchise given by the second Reform Act, passed in 1867, applied only to male voters, increasing the number of men eligible to vote by 1 million to 2 million – there was still no sign of votes for women.

The organisation of support for women's votes was quick to arrive in Birmingham, aided by the existence of close networks of family and friends who were already interested and actively involved in various social justice campaigns. A newly-arrived resident to the city, Unitarian businessman William Taylor, his wife Caroline and their young family (son Peter and daughters Catherine and Edith), set up home at 10 Chad Road in Edgbaston: William's brother was Peter Alfred Taylor, whose wife, Clementia, was now secretary of the newly-established London Suffrage Society. Clementia had written to her sister-in-law, urging Caroline and Miss Mary Johnson (of Wheeleys Road, and an early subscriber to the London committee) to set up a branch in Birmingham, and so, on 21 April 1868 the Birmingham Women's Suffrage Society was formally established.[16] William and Caroline were executive committee members (Caroline later became Treasurer in 1871), while Mary Johnson acted as Secretary. The formation of political societies was often reliant on family connections and networks of mutual interests, in this case, extending outwards from activity in London and Manchester. Birmingham was seen as an important addition, given the city's previous experience of political and social justice campaigning demonstrated by the Chartist and abolition of slavery movements.[17] The first public meeting of the newly-formed Society was held at the Exchange Assembly Rooms on New Street.

On 25 April 1868 *The Birmingham Journal* reported the Society's formation: 'the committee are arranging for a public meeting to take place shortly, for the purpose of getting signatures to a petition to be laid before Parliament in May, praying that widows and single women fulfilling the conditions of property or occupancy required of men, should not be deprived of the franchise on account of sex'. The franchise was not being sought for all women but for unmarried women who qualified on the same basis as men. Legally, a married woman's rights were subsumed into those of her husband, thereby encouraging the argument that it was unnecessary for married women to have the right to vote. However, legislation that was about to be passed signalled gradual change. The Married Women's Property Act of 1870 would allow any money that a woman earned to be treated as her own property and not that of her husband's.

The *Englishwoman's Review* described the meeting at the Exchange held on 8 May as 'crowded and the enthusiasm great'.[18] Birmingham, that 'stronghold of Liberal non-conformity', and a city proficient in organising political campaigns was now ready to work towards gaining votes for women.[19] *The Birmingham Journal* on 9 May further elaborated on the meeting and the speeches given conveyed a sense of excitement and optimism at the setting up of a campaigning organisation in the city with support from people like John Stuart Mill. Although unable to attend the meeting, Mill had sent a letter of apology in which he asserted, 'there is no movement to which I should be more happy to devote my time and labour than to this one, the consequences of which are likely to be so momentous and so beneficial to both sexes'. The Chairman, the Venerable Archdeacon Sandford, said that 'he believed women would exercise the franchise for the best interests of society'. Miss Robertson, one of the committee members, addressed the meeting and remarked, 'the idea that women had nothing to do with politics was fast giving way... Politics so frequently affected the minutest particulars of household life and economy, that it could not be denied that women should take an interest in such affairs'. Although public speaking, and the possibility of having to deal with vocal responses of audience members, could be intimidating for women who were new to political campaigning, their participation in public meetings and lectures was essential in conveying the arguments of the suffrage societies to the wider public and, in turn, encouraging more women to join the movement.

A petition that had been instigated by the Society, the first one to come specifically from the city, had been signed by 905 residents of Birmingham and was presented to Parliament by the reformer John Bright, MP for Birmingham, on 28 May, 'praying for the extension of the Suffrage to Women, fulfilling the condition of property or occupancy required of men'.[20] John Stuart Mill had managed to convince a sceptical Bright to support the women's suffrage amendment, although Bright would later vote against it in 1876. Despite the evident success of the May meeting, an article in *The Birmingham Journal* raised doubts about how legitimately it could claim to represent Birmingham and questioned where the speakers at the meeting had come from.[21] This was refuted the following week by the secretary, Mary Johnson: 'the meeting was originated and promoted solely by the Birmingham committee… That out of the eight gentleman speakers, four were Birmingham men; and that the platform, with the exception of four gentlemen and two ladies, was entirely occupied by Birmingham men and women'. The mixed-sex membership of the suffrage societies and the support of men was necessary at this time to encourage parliamentary debate, although this policy would not be adopted by later militant activists. By October there was no doubt that the campaign for women's votes had arrived in earnest in Birmingham. The *Englishwoman's Review* noted that it had received the first half-yearly report of the BWSS, observing that 'it began with a very small committee but there are now forty ladies and gentlemen on the general committee, and the movement continues to acquire strength'.[22]

Only two years after the formation of the BWSS, the first dedicated women's suffrage Bill was brought to Parliament in 1870 by Jacob Bright, Radical Liberal MP for Manchester and brother of John (their sister, Priscilla Bright McLaren was involved in anti-slavery and women's suffrage campaigning in Edinburgh). Jacob Bright had been present at the first meeting of the Manchester Suffrage Society and had helped achieve a major step in the fight for women's equality in 1869 by helping to secure the right for women to vote in municipal elections. Although Bright's 1870 women's suffrage amendment was unsuccessful, it did galvanise the movement and activists continued to organise petitions, hold public meetings and lobby MPs. In 1869 Eliza Mary Sturge became Secretary of the BWSS, after Mary Johnson moved away from the city. Like the Taylors, Sturge was a reformer, immersed in politics from a young age and influenced by the activist members of her family. Her aunt, Sophia, was present at the meeting to establish the Birmingham Ladies Society for the Relief of Negro Slaves, and her uncle, Joseph, was a celebrated anti-slavery campaigner. Eliza herself would dedicate her life to liberal causes.

On 5 December 1871 a suffrage meeting was held at the Masonic Hall and a long article in the *Birmingham Daily Post* the following day titled 'Woman's Suffrage' described the proceedings. Many important speakers were in attendance, from Birmingham and further afield. Millicent Garrett Fawcett, one of the members of the

London Society for Women's Suffrage, was present, as were the great and the good of Birmingham's social and political circles: the preacher, lecturer and activist George Dawson chaired the meeting; also there were the Liberal politicians George Dixon and John Middlemore, Eliza Sturge, William and Caroline Taylor, and the Reverend Crosskey, pastor of the Church of the Messiah on Broad Street. Dawson opened the meeting by asking 'ought the fact of women being women to disqualify them for the exercise of the privilege which the law had attached to property?' Crosskey proposed the resolution 'that the ownership or occupation of land and houses being the basis of representation in this country, it is unjust in principle to make sex a ground for disqualification, hereby excluding a large number of intelligent persons well qualified to exercise the electoral franchise'.

The resolution was seconded by Eliza Sturge who went on to rebut the reasons that were typically given against women's votes. The most popular argument against it was based on the theory of separate spheres for men and women. This put forward the notion that 'if women claimed equality with men they would lose their present influence, and forfeit their claim to the respect and deference with which they had hitherto been regarded'. For Sturge, this deference paid to women was entirely false and had been founded on social fictions. The notion of a 'woman's sphere' was 'only a remnant of astrological superstition... When words needed saying and deeds needed doing, were women to sit down and talk about their "spheres"?' Sturge was then loudly applauded as she declared that 'until women took their right position, the highest stage either of social or national life would not be reached, and therefore with heart and soul she supported the cause of women's suffrage'. Millicent Fawcett was also cheered as she took the floor to support the resolution and urged men who had been given the vote after the 1867 Reform Act not to 'push down the ladder which you ascended... apply your arguments to the women'. The resolution was carried with only four dissentients.[23] Despite parliamentary failure in winning votes for women, it was clear that the grassroots movement was strengthening and was being led in the city by strong, intelligent and capable women, well versed in the politics of reform and social justice and more than able to put forward a convincing argument for extending the franchise.

Millicent Fawcett returned to Birmingham the following year on 6 December 1872 for a meeting at the Town Hall, which was chaired by George Dixon. In this year the BWSS had affiliated itself with the Central Committee of the National Society for Women's Suffrage, of which Fawcett was a member. In her address to the assembled crowd, Fawcett acknowledged Birmingham's reforming past and urged again that those who had fought for extending the franchise to working men must now aid women in their fight. This time she stated, 'I can scarcely imagine that the Birmingham politicians, who took so prominent a part in the reform agitation for the extension of the suffrage to working men, can be blind to the patent fact that all the most convincing arguments used during that agitation in favour of admitting the working classes to representation apply with equal cogency to the case of women'.[24] The city's three MPs at the time were Dixon, John Bright and Philip Henry Muntz, who had been a member of the Chartist delegation in 1838. That year a speech given by Eliza Sturge at the Town Hall, 'On Women's Suffrage', was published as a pamphlet, allowing the message to be spread further afield to those who had not been present to hear her talk.

In 1873 Eliza's hard work and dedication to civic causes paid off as she became the first woman elected to the Birmingham School Board. This had been made possible by the passing of the Education Act in 1870, which allowed women to vote for School Boards and also to run as candidates to serve on the Boards. Eliza's achievements were acknowledged in a speech that Caroline Taylor gave in January 1874 at a National Suffrage Society conference which took place in Birmingham at the Midland Institute. Caroline recognised that while Birmingham still had work to do in terms of being recognised as a campaigning city for women's enfranchisement, 'it had made for itself in the past year a claim to be considered a fitting centre for such a gathering as they were holding'. For Caroline, the efforts of Eliza Sturge were of immense benefit to the city and to the campaign: 'In no great town in England had there been of late years more convincing proof that women could and did take an active interest in public movements than had been shown by the action of the women of Birmingham in the School Board election of last autumn. The difficult work undertaken, arranged, and carried out by women in that election – namely, the personal canvass of all the women ratepayers of the town – was a proof of the deep interest felt by them in the political struggle brought to such a successful termination.'[25]

While there was much to celebrate and build upon, the peculiarity of having a vote in some areas but not others was pointed out by Caroline, who observed that 'it would seem obvious to any thoughtful mind that the state of the present law of representation, which allowed women to participate in the measure which affected the welfare of children, and which denied to them any voice in the formation of laws which affected themselves, was an anomaly which no argument could uphold nor justice sanction'. It was clear to her and to others involved in the campaign that this argument was nonsensical and unsustainable. She continued, 'they were told by their opponents that women were fully represented by men: but if such were the case how were they to account for the unjust laws in force against women at the present time? The time was, they believed, gone by when women would be stigmatised as "stepping out of their sphere" if they took an interest in broad social questions or in matters beyond the household circle'.[26] Six years after establishing the BWSS the impatience and frustration felt at the double standards applied to women and dissatisfaction at the disadvantaged position in which women found themselves was clear. However, the burgeoning success of the Society was confirmed by the opening in 1874 of an office at 4 Broad Street Corner, where members could hold meetings and distribute pamphlets. A few years later the campaign received a blow when in 1878, Eliza Sturge left Birmingham, although she remained secretary for the BWSS until 1885. However, this period in the late 1870s, ten years on from Mill's petition, demonstrates that although there were still many frustrations, persistence was beginning to pay off. More women were starting to step out of 'the woman's sphere', and become involved in social and civic causes. While clearly an exciting time, it also gives a sense of how much hard work they needed to be prepared to do, and the sheer dedication to the cause demonstrated by those at its forefront.

In April 1877 another conference was held in the city, on this occasion in support of Jacob Bright moving another women's suffrage Bill, which, had it been successful, would have added 300,000 women to the franchise. The conference was reported in the *Birmingham Daily Post* on 18 April: during the meeting a motion was moved by the Reverend Crosskey 'that the exclusion of women householders and ratepayers, legally qualified in every respect but that of sex, from the power of voting in the election of members of Parliament, by depriving a considerable portion of the property, the industry, and the intelligence of the country of all direct representation, is injurious both to the person excluded and to the community at large'. The motion was seconded by the BWSS treasurer Catherine Courtauld Osler, eldest daughter of Caroline and William Taylor, who urged that women be given more freedom to participate in society, in order to protect their rights and interests: 'it was a mere hollow pretence to say that women could be properly represented by men… If women were admitted to the Parliamentary franchise they would put an end to some of the injustices which the laws imposed upon them… As to the franchise unsexing women, she was not aware that the voting for School Boards had unsexed them: and what reasonable expectation could there be that voting for borough members would bring about that effect?'[27]

From a wealthy and privileged family, living in an affluent area of the city, Catherine Taylor – now Osler – had grown up in the midst of liberal politics and social justice campaigning, surrounded by strong women activists. When the BWSS was established Catherine, aged 14, was one of the first subscribers and would go on to become one of the suffrage movement's key Birmingham leaders. After marrying the glass manufacturer Alfred Osler in 1873, the family first lived at 44 Wheeleys Road and then moved to a larger house, 'Fallowfield' on Norfolk Road in Edgbaston. Like many wealthy liberal young women, Catherine was able to take an active role in politics and public life and, as well as her involvement in suffrage campaigning, she later became President of the Birmingham Women's Liberal Association. Being so close to such impressive female role models early on would have had an impact on Catherine as she became increasingly involved in civic life: not only did her mother set an early example of the hard work required but Catherine would have witnessed the dedication and enthusiasm of Eliza Sturge, only twelve years her senior, and she was present at the many speeches given in the city in the 1870s by Millicent Fawcett, who would go on to become a life-long friend. As we have seen, both Eliza Sturge and Caroline Taylor were instrumental in the running of the Birmingham Society, their lives spent busily writing articles and giving public addresses to large groups of people. Alongside these outstanding examples of female achievement, however, Catherine would also have witnessed a world in which women were being constantly told that their place was in a separate sphere to that of men and that they were not to be trusted with something as serious as the vote.

Suffrage meetings continued into the new decade and February 1881 saw a 'great demonstration' at the Town Hall, in support of the Liberal MP Hugh Mason's resolution in favour of the extension of the franchise to women householders.[28] To enable more women to come to the meeting, they were allowed free entry while gentlemen had to buy tickets for the galleries at 2s. 6d. The Reverend Crosskey's wife presided over a crowded hall and Catherine Osler was present along with her mother, Caroline. Also present was a Mrs W. H. Ryland, another affluent Edgbaston resident, who lived not far from the Osler family home, on St Augustine's Road (they would later move to 19 Hermitage Road, also in Edgbaston). Alice Ryland was married to William Henry Ryland, a surveyor. William's cousin, Frederick Ryland, was married to Clara Chamberlain, sister of Joseph, at that time President of the Board of Trade. Alice would soon become pregnant with her fifth child, Bertha, who would go on to follow her mother into suffrage politics, although of the more militant persuasion. In addition to the main meeting, 19 smaller meetings were held in wards and board schools in the weeks leading up to the Town Hall demonstration and an overflow meeting had to be set up at the nearby YMCA because of the large numbers of attendees, in spite of inclement weather.

The following year saw the passing of the 1882 Married Women's Property Act which extended the 1870 Act and now recognised a wife's legal identity and the right to own, buy, and sell her own property. The Courts would also now have to recognise a husband and wife as two separate legal identities. The suffrage societies still advocated votes for unmarried women on the same basis as men, however. Although it seemed that progress was being made, in January 1883 at another suffrage meeting at the Town Hall, Catherine Osler's frustration at the lack of progress despite the huge turnout two years before was clear and she complained about the 'indifference which was evinced by the general public and members of Parliament towards the women's suffrage movement'.[29] The meeting had also received a letter of apology from Joseph Chamberlain, who had been an MP for the city since 1876. While agreeing that there were many women who deserved the vote, Chamberlain remarked that the practical advantages of extending the franchise must first be established. In response, Mrs Ashford, senior BWSS committee member, pointed out, with understandable annoyance, that she did not remember men being 'asked to show what advantages would accrue if the franchise was extended to them'. 1884 saw the passing of a third Reform Act, supported by Chamberlain, which extended the electorate to include over five million men although 40% of working-class men still did not have the right to vote.

The BWSS annual report for 1885 noted that a canvass of women householders in the city had 'obtained a large proportion of their signatures to a petition in favour of Mr Woodall's Bill (extending the Parliamentary Franchise to Women)'.[30] However, this amendment was killed off after Prime Minister William Gladstone made it clear that he did not support it, fearful that women voters, property-owning and wealthy, would side with the Conservative Party. The protection of personal and party interests by male politicians was to block women's suffrage for many years to come. A general election that same year returned Gladstone's Liberal Party but with a reduced minority. The following year another petition from Birmingham was presented to Parliament by George Dixon, this time with 4,707 signatures, an impressive increase on the four who had signed Mill's petition twenty years earlier. This gave the BWSS cause for optimism and they remarked in their annual report, 'the present epoch is, however, one of such rapidly successive political crises that legislation has only proceeded by snatched opportunities, and it is felt that no definite expectations with regard to any measure can be entertained, while any day may bring a change in the Government of the country or even a dissolution of Parliament'. Not only was the present political uncertainty reason for hope but 'a noticeable feature in the General Election of 1885 was the very active part taken on both sides by women… It is obvious that women are taking, and will take, an increasing share in the active work of politics; and the question which is still to some extent in the power of our legislators to decide, is whether this share shall be of a direct and authorized nature as opposed to what has been sometimes called a "backstairs influence".[31] After the Liberals had failed to secure a majority in Parliament, another election took place the following year and saw the Conservative Party take power, helped by an electoral pact with Joseph Chamberlain's breakaway Unionist wing of the Liberal Party.

Although there were reasons to feel optimistic, the late 1880s was a period of painfully slow progress and, while there were enough supportive MPs to put forward bills or amendments, there was not the wider support to secure a second reading. In the BWSS report for 1888 the same frustration around women being able to vote in some municipal elections while still not being permitted to vote in general elections was evident. The willingness of women to serve civic society was clear and it was noted in the report that the Liberal Association's Annual Election placed 23 women on the party's General Council and four on the Executive Committee, but dismay at the position that women found themselves in was strongly felt: 'All this can have but one issue. That women will be satisfied to give their time, talent, labour, and thought to political work, and yet remain legally political nonentities, is neither to be expected nor desired. To suppose that men of any party could be so lost to all sense of justice and honour as to accept the labour of women in public life whilst denying them its privilege, would be to offer an insult to English manliness. The present condition of things is anomalous to absurdity. In Birmingham at the present time women can and do sit on the Divisional Councils, which declare the policy of the Parliamentary constituencies and select their candidates, for whom, when they are chosen, not a single woman may vote.' However, the Society wanted its members to feel optimistic: 'notwithstanding the unfavourable attitude of some of the Members for Birmingham (once friendly to our cause), your committee feel that the general sentiment of the country is with us: that the women's political organisations which are constantly growing in numbers and importance all over the country are educating their members rapidly, not only to a real interest in politics, but to the perception of their own urgent need for representation'.[32]

While the movement for women's suffrage seemed to be strengthening, fractures within the national organisation began to appear and in 1888 the Central Committee of the National Society for Women's Suffrage split. This was related to disputes within the Liberal Party – the main bone of contention was disagreement over whether the rules should be changed to allow other political organisations to affiliate, the concern being that the Suffrage Society would be joined by members of the Women's Liberal Federation, which supported Gladstone and Home Rule for Ireland (the Oslers were included in this faction). There were also other troubling issues: disagreements about how to deal with the Contagious Diseases Act (Osler supported its repeal); the reluctance of some in the provinces to accept leadership from London (although this does not seem to apply to Birmingham, Osler and Fawcett remained on friendly terms despite disagreeing over Home Rule); and divisions over whether to support legislation that gave single women the vote but excluded married women. After the split, the Home Rulers formed the Central National Society for Women's Suffrage while Fawcett led a reconstituted Central Committee of the National Society for Women's Suffrage. As Elizabeth Crawford has observed, 'for most of the 1890s the suffrage movement rather lost its focus, although individual members and societies were extremely active'.[33] Indeed, in the 1890s the BWSS continued to meet frequently. A letter to the *Birmingham Daily Post* from the Reverend Crosskey and the two Taylor sisters, Catherine Osler and Edith Reid, now treasurer after Catherine became secretary in 1885, celebrated the longevity of the Society, which had now been running for over 20 years: 'in respect of age, therefore, it must be acknowledged that it compares favourably with any political movement of this century, and can hardly be said not to have received a sufficient amount of public attention to entitle it to a forward place among the questions of the day'.[34]

The biennial BWSS meeting on 11 June 1890 was reported in the *Birmingham Daily Post*: the quiet confidence of the Society was evident and here the Reverend Crosskey asserted that 'it was now no longer possible for their society to be the subject of the kind of ridicule that it was years ago. It now stood in the position of having every argument held against it absolutely answered, and there only remained that kind of agitation which appeared to be necessary to carry any great principle into practice'. In the early days of suffrage campaigning John Stuart Mill had been subject to much ridicule in Parliament and in the newspapers when raising the issue. While, by the 1890s, suffrage campaigners could argue against their opponents with increasing confidence, it did not stop those determined to fight against the suffragists. The previous year an 'Appeal Against Female Suffrage' had been signed by over 100 women, which then later increased to over 2,000 signatures after publication in *The Nineteenth Century* magazine. This was the first collective protest by women against women's suffrage, although it did not lead to any formal organisation. The article appealed to 'common sense and educated thought' and the main argument against women's votes reinforced the idea of separate spheres. The author of the article, Mrs Humphrey Ward, stated that although they accepted and encouraged the education and development of women, it should be restricted to matters dealing with children, health and welfare, and that women's work must remain separate from the business of Parliament, understood as the realm of men only.[35]

The speech by Crosskey was his last as President before his death in 1893 and this would signal an important shift within the BWSS. At the meeting Catherine Osler spoke 'in praise of the valuable services rendered by Dr Crosskey' but also urged female members that 'they must not look to men to win their freedom for them: they must fight their battles for themselves'. From then on the leadership of the Society was completely female. The Society also wanted to encourage new members. The annual report for 1892 urged 'what our Birmingham Society now chiefly needs is the help of young and active supporters, who will come forward to sustain and in due time relieve those who for so many years have carried on the work. The more our younger workers associate themselves in philanthropic, charitable, and educational interests, the more they must feel the need of the direct influence of women in the making of the laws of our country. In this way we have won and shall continue to win many adherents, for Birmingham is full of generous and unselfish workers, who have only to realise the true aims and scope of the reform for which we are labouring, to give us their warm sympathy and active co-operation'. Although there was much to celebrate, including the continued work of the Society and the dedication of its members, by the end of the century almost 60% of adult males could vote while women were still prevented from holding that democratic right. In direct terms, women were no further on in their fight for the vote on the same terms as men than they had been in the 1860s.

The frustration continues

The 1890s saw attempts within the national suffrage movement to regroup. The BWSS had managed to maintain an independent position during the split and worked 'whenever opportunity offered, in friendly conjunction with either or both of the London societies'. The 1892 report also observed: 'When we calmly consider the position of our movement today, especially as regards its prominence and importance in the estimation of the country generally, we have assuredly every encouragement to stand steadily to our purpose, and press forward with renewed hope and courage to its speedy realisation.'[36] It seemed the time was now right to establish a united national organisation again. On 16 October 1896 a conference of the two suffrage organisations, the National Central Society and the Central Committee, was held at the Priory Schools in Birmingham, and the following year, in 1897, the National Union for Women's Suffrage Societies was officially formed under the leadership of Millicent Fawcett. As we have seen, Birmingham was a popular destination for meetings of national organisations, most likely due to its central location, ease of transport from London and other parts of the country, and because of its reputation as a reform city, but also because now the BWSS was under the strong leadership and organisation of Mrs Ashford, who had become President after the death of Dr Crosskey in 1893, ably assisted by Catherine Osler and Edith Reid.

At the meeting it was resolved that each local branch should 'undertake a definite area of the UK, thus more effectively to extend the woman's suffrage movement', and urged that 'women of each political party should abstain from working for or assisting in any way those Parliamentary candidates who do not declare themselves in favour of the extension of the Parliamentary franchise to all duly qualified women'.[37] The NUWSS would work towards the education of the public in an attempt to convince or change opinion and organise pressure within parliamentary constituencies, and would set up branches to focus on lobbying their elected representatives. There is a clear sense at this time that the organisation, both on a national and local level, was being thought about more seriously and more strategically, and that members were more determined than ever, giving the movement fresh impetus. Towards the end of the century it looked as though progress might finally be made and in 1897 a private-member women's suffrage Bill passed a second reading for the first time, although it was later defeated. The Bill was supported in Birmingham by the MPs George Dixon, Jesse Collings and Benjamin Stone. Joseph Chamberlain and his son Austen, now MP for East Worcestershire, both voted against the resolution.[38]

Despite the failure of the 1897 Bill, in October 1900 the minutes of the Birmingham Society record that one of its best ever drawing-room meetings had been held in a private house at which 100 ladies were present and 26 new members enrolled.[39] In 1901 Catherine Osler succeeded Mrs Ashford to become President of the BWSS. As Crawford describes it, the suffrage campaign in Birmingham at this time was very much 'an Edgbaston affair', dominated by 'local prominent liberals, involved in the civic gospel, often Unitarians committed to typical Liberal causes', many of them part of the same social circles.[40] Indeed, the wider political elite in Birmingham was a close-knit group, formerly comprising adherents of George Dawson's civic gospel and now made up of men of business, industry and Empire, dominated by the Chamberlain family.[41] Subscribers to the BWSS included well-known names within the city, for example, Mrs George Cadbury, Mrs Southall and Miss Sturge. As before, constitutional methods were adhered to – petitions were signed, 'At-Home' meetings and public debates were held, leaflets were distributed, and deputations to Parliament were organised. Progress was still slow, however.

Momentum had been disrupted by the Boer War of 1898-1902,[42] and the BWSS annual report for 1902-3 noted that 'although direct Parliamentary progress cannot this year be recorded, yet there is much cause for clear indications here given that time and experience are working on our side'. The Society continued to expand and new branches were opened across the Midlands.

Although the suffrage movement in Birmingham was led by members of the Edgbaston elite, concern for the welfare of women of all classes was felt by many involved in the campaign. In the report for the year 1903-4 the Society revealed that the 'committee, after careful consideration, thought it advisable early in the winter to undertake some work among working women on the lines of that done among the textile workers of Lancashire and the North. It was decided to begin with the chain makers of Cradley Heath[43] and the surrounding districts'.[44] The Society even invited Esther Roper and Eva Gore-Booth, members of the Manchester Suffrage Society who had both carried out successful work in promoting the unions, to come and talk to the Cradley Heath workers. Both women had been instrumental in collecting a textile workers' petition in 1901 and 1902, which 'led Roper and Gore-Booth to establish in 1903 a new suffrage society, the Lancashire and Cheshire Textile and Other Workers Representation Committee, to build on this movement. In contrast to the NUWSS, 'the Lancashire and Cheshire committee campaigned for full womanhood suffrage, a demand that signalled a commitment to a fully democratic franchise alongside recognition of the particular disabilities of women'.[45]

Industrial employment accounted for approximately two thirds of female employment in Birmingham at the end of the 19th century. The 1901 census showed that in Birmingham 38% of the total female population over ten years of age were in work, although this would have been paid employment and would not have taken into consideration women working from home, doing jobs such as sewing and taking in extra washing. The largest majority of employed women worked in minerals, metals and mines and nearly 7 out of 10 women were employed in industrial occupations by this time.[46] Catherine Osler had been involved in improving conditions for working women since the 1890s, chairing a meeting in November 1890 at the annual gathering of the Birmingham Ladies Union of Workers. This middle-class-dominated organisation was powerful enough in Birmingham to sustain from 1891 to 1924 a quarterly magazine called *Women Workers*, of which the BWSS was an affiliated organisation. In 1904 a study was undertaken by Edward Cadbury, Cecile Matheson and George Shann into the conditions of working women, published as *Women's Work and Wages* (1904-7).[47] Their report included an analysis of the wages of 6,000 Birmingham women, which revealed that the average wage, calculated for married women working in a multitude of grades, came to 9/1d per week – this was less than the subsistence level.[48] As demonstrated by the Female Political Union in the early part of the 19th century, the fight for the vote was intertwined with the fight to improve women's lives.

Progress in securing the vote for women had gained strength throughout the 19th century but it was painfully slow. By the turn of the new century the patience of many had run out and, in response, a new organisation was formed in 1903 in Manchester, the Women's Social & Political Union (WSPU), established by Emmeline Pankhurst and her two daughters, Christabel and Sylvia, at their family home. This was to be a women-only organisation, initially connected to the Independent Labour Party (ILP), of which Emmeline Pankhurst was a member, and would campaign, like the NUWSS, for votes for women on the same basis as men. As the ILP became the Labour Party most of its members wanted to focus on securing the vote for working class men and saw women's suffrage as a secondary issue, resulting in the WSPU actively opposing both them and Liberal candidates, although Labour members such as George Lansbury, Philip Snowden and Keir Hardie were passionate advocates of giving women the vote. Though the introduction of private members Bills was now happening on a yearly basis, Emmeline Pankhurst saw these as futile and so she undertook the first protest at Parliament in 1905, loudly demonstrating outside after another women's suffrage Bill was rejected. This, along with Christabel Pankhurst and Annie Kenney's disruption of a Liberal Party meeting at Manchester's Free Trade Hall and their subsequent arrest later that year, signalled the beginning of 'militant' action or civil disobedience in pursuit of publicising the cause. Women's suffrage would begin to join other political issues, such as Irish Nationalism, filling the papers of the time with stories of violent action. 1906, the year of a General Election, saw the WSPU move its headquarters to London, leading to a different way of managing the campaign from a central control, with organisers being appointed by the leadership and then sent out to the regions. This was the start of militancy proper and activity quickly spread across the country, including to Birmingham.

The beginnings of militancy in the city: 1906-1909

'Birmingham is about to become one of the strongholds of the movement'

Votes for Women, November 1907

A new dawn?

1906 began with a landslide election victory for the Liberal Party, led by Henry Campbell-Bannerman, ousting the Unionist Government that had been formed in 1895. Constitutional suffragists continued their campaign for votes for women as they had been doing since the 1870s, focusing on education of the public and lobbying of MPs. Although they would differ tactically, both the NUWSS and WSPU wanted the vote for women on the same terms as men (as determined by the property qualification), as opposed to the vote for all adult women: although some suffragists did advocate full womanhood suffrage, this was a radical demand at that time. While the militants attempted to send groups of women to Parliament to meet with ministers, their main tactic was to interrupt political meetings, an action that, for some commentators, precisely justified the reasons why women should not be given the vote. Although officially the NUWSS did not agree with these new tactics, it did not yet go as far as to condemn them, and, indeed, could see the reasons for it. Catherine Osler, in a letter to *The Spectator* referring to the most recent NUWSS Parliamentary delegation, described the double standard that applied to women, observing that 'we must conform to tests and satisfy requirements never imposed on [men]'. She also went as far as defending the frustration felt by the militants and argued against the reaction it had provoked, which was, to her mind, quite understandable: 'yet when, after a longer peaceful agitation and a superior patience to that shown by other classes, some women are at last betraying exasperation at the obstinate refusal of their just demands, an argument is often deduced from their loss of self-control against their fitness for citizenship'.[49]

While not wholly unamenable to women voters, the new Prime Minister rather unhelpfully advised that the women should continue to pester Government until they succeeded (many suffragists would have argued that they had spent the past thirty years pestering politicians). Indeed, this was remarked upon in the BWSS report for 1905-6, which discussed the NUWSS deputation of 350 delegates sent to meet Campbell-

Bannerman: 'the reply of the PM was distinctly disappointing. He committed himself deeply and irrevocably as regards his own personal opinion, but gave no promise whatever of any definite help either in the near or distant future, but merely urged the exercise of further patience and the education of public opinion'. Despite expressing some understanding of the militants' position, the annual BWSS report for 1905-6 demonstrated impatience with the tactics now being employed and perhaps some concern at the impact interrupting politicians in public meetings might have on the wider campaign: 'it cannot be too deeply regretted that an opportunity so likely to yield a favourable division should have been lost by the ill-judged and regrettable behaviour of certain extreme women suffragists, unconnected with the official organisation. The interruption of meetings which occurred during the Election and later… have done harm to the cause, and no one has more reason to deplore these occurrences than the NUWSS'. By 1906, the activities of the WSPU had gained enough press attention for the *Daily Mail* to coin the word 'suffragette', a derogatory phrase intended to distinguish these new militants from their constitutional counterparts but one that WSPU appropriated and embraced. Indeed, the importance of being front page news was something that they were acutely aware of and they actively exploited this throughout their campaign.

In this first decade of the new century, private members' Bills continued to be brought before Parliament but to no avail, including one in February 1907 which reached a second reading but ran out of time before it could be made into law. This Bill was remarkable in that it would have included 'women wherever the masculine gender is used as qualification for voters; and it also provided that a woman should not be disqualified by marriage'.[50] Although a supporter of widening the franchise, arguing 'that there should be no taxation without direct representation', Campbell-Bannerman disliked the Bill 'which would enfranchise a minority of well-to-do women', who, he thought, would be potential Conservative Party voters.[51] The ways in which women would vote was a consideration for politicians, each political party fearing that the enfranchisement of women could mean electoral defeat for them, and both Liberals and Conservatives thought women would vote against them while some in the Labour Party were suspicious of a campaign that was led largely by middle-class women. Other arguments against women voting were also presented. In addition to being unsuited or unfit to vote, in an article titled 'Female Suffrage', *The Spectator* gave the reason that the union between men and women would be 'endangered by a division, and so a clash of authority, between the sexes' if women were allowed to vote. The article continued, 'if… political authority is given to women – and if it is given at all it must be given on the same terms as to men –

that conflict is always a menacing possibility'. This prospect of men and women 'sharing authority' was, for some, unthinkable.[52]

Again, Catherine Osler responded by letter to the editor of *The Spectator*, expressing her incredulity that 'we are asked today to resume the position of half a century ago, and to declare that the convictions and opinions of one half of humanity can only be tolerated by the other half so long as they are deprived of any practical effectiveness'.[53] While the constant stalemate and seeming lack of progress over the past four decades in the fight for the vote meant that many women were growing impatient with the NUWSS, its membership continued to grow during this time and, in the Midlands, as well as the central branch in Birmingham, there were also branches established in Wolverhampton, Stourbridge, Wednesbury and West Bromwich. During 1907 the Society held 30 meetings in Birmingham and the surrounding district and by the following year the amount of subscriptions made it the second largest Society in England after London.[54] The women of Birmingham were clearly not in the mood to back down from fighting for the cause.

For Mrs Pankhurst private members' Bills were perceived as a waste of time, and so more forceful action was now required – the motto 'Deeds not Words' was quickly adopted as the WSPU campaign slogan. In addition to the public protests carried out by members of the Union, the organisation also began publishing its own newspaper, *Votes for Women (Votes for Women)*, in October 1907, allowing it to make a case for female enfranchisement on a weekly basis along with sharing news from across the country. The newspaper was edited by Emmeline Pethick Lawrence,[55] WSPU treasurer, with her husband, Frederick Pethick Lawrence. It was dedicated 'To the brave women who today are fighting for freedom: to the noble women who all down the ages kept the flag flying and looked forward to this day without seeing it: to all women all over the world of whatever race, creed, or calling, whether they be with us or against us in this fight'. The WSPU also now worked hard to establish local branch offices, appointing organisers to lead campaigns locally. Work began in Birmingham in 1906 when Mary Gawthorpe, a WSPU member from the north of England, was sent to the Midlands by the Pankhursts, although her attempts to garner support were not straightforward: Gawthorpe remarked that the city was 'a hard nut to crack', and the lack of sympathetic colleagues and the vastness of the city was reportedly challenging for her.[56] This may have been due to the dominance of the BWSS, led by local Birmingham people, and there was perhaps suspicion of an outsider sent to launch militancy in the city. However, this proved to be a short-lived problem and by October 1907 local efforts were beginning to pay off: it was reported in *Votes for Women* on 17 October that 'an energetic campaign is in progress in Birmingham. One of the national organisers, Miss Nell Kenney, is in the city, and the local members are giving her every assistance in preparing for the great Town Hall demonstration on November 20', at which leaders Emmeline and Christabel Pankhurst and Emmeline Pethick Lawrence would address the meeting.[57]

A WSPU 'At-Home' gathering was held at the Grand Hotel on Colmore Row on the same evening as the Town Hall meeting, where 'several representative women have accepted our invitation to be present, and we hope that the local movement will be much strengthened as a result of this gathering'. It was proclaimed in *Votes for Women* that 'Birmingham, we believe, is about to become one of the strongholds of our movement'. In addition to larger-scale meetings at the Town Hall, lots of other activity was taking place, including talks at Aston and Selly Oak Co-operative Guilds, and meetings at works typically held outside the factory gates on dinner hours, including Kynochs, Dunlop and Brompton. Nell Kenney, now leading the campaign in the city, elaborated on activities in her weekly update: 'the local committee are beginning a visiting campaign among their own members, and I am visiting most of the influential people in Birmingham and surrounding districts. Our meetings are run on strictly economical lines. The outdoor meetings are being advertised by chalking the pavements or ringing the bell, and the audiences so far have been orderly and sympathetic'.[58]

This new militant organisation was viewed by constitutional suffragists, many of whom had been involved in the campaign for decades, as a development led by a different generation who were set on employing disruptive tactics, which the constitutional campaigners remained unconvinced would be successful. The BWSS report for this period observed in an article about the WSPU 'that the question of Woman's Suffrage has become one of practical politics and of everyday discussion is, no doubt, largely due to the militant tactics of the WSPU, but it still remains to be proved whether their advocacy of the cause will on the whole do harm or good. Their zeal and self-sacrifice has aroused and inspired with enthusiasm an immense number of hitherto indifferent onlookers, both men and women: but the particular methods employed have undeniably alienated many old supporters'.[59] Indeed, even within the WSPU there were those who remained unconvinced, both by the choice of tactics and by the autocratic style of leadership. In 1907 another organisation was set up, the Women's Freedom League, by former WSPU members, although the group never took off in Birmingham.

The new method of interrupting political meetings that had been adopted by the militants continued to be publicly discussed. In December 1907 a debate was held at the

University of Birmingham. Sir Oliver Lodge, Principal of the University, had challenged undergraduates to a joint debate with the WSPU after the recent meeting at the Town Hall had been disrupted by student hecklers. Lodge had been a long term advocate of votes for women. In an address at the BWSS's annual meeting in 1902, he commented that 'it is a highly artificial disqualification to disenfranchise property because it is owned or occupied by a woman', and called the withholding of the vote from women 'a gratuitous insult'.[60] Christabel Pankhurst was present at the University meeting in 1907 and the motion was submitted 'that the methods of the WSPU are best calculated to advance the cause of women's suffrage'. It was reported in *Votes for Women* that the meeting was 'attended by a very large number of undergraduates. A large proportion of those voting against the resolution were youths who appeared to object to the aims, as well as to the methods, of our Union, and to dislike strongly the idea of women enjoying fair play in political and social life'.[61] One of the undergraduates opposed the motion, remarking that the women had not convinced the British public to take them seriously and that their methods were merely amusing rather than intimidating.

Any fears that politicians or members of the public may have had about the extreme lengths the women might be prepared to go to were confirmed by Christabel Pankhurst's provocative statement that while the women did not want to go further just at present, they were prepared to do so if they felt it necessary. She concluded that the tactics were there, whether people liked them or not, and if they did not like them, then they should give women the franchise. Unfortunately a large majority, including many of the women present, voted against the motion.[62] The following year, Lodge wrote an article for the University's student paper, *The Mermaid*, in which he again argued that there was no justification in excluding women from the franchise based on a property qualification, and stated that it was 'absurd that an otherwise complete qualification for political activity should be neutralised solely by the sex of the responsible and taxpaying owner or occupier, thus inflicting an offensive and totally underserved stigma on half the human race'. He also refuted arguments of political illiteracy among women. Lodge went on to discuss the tactics now being used by the suffragettes, of which he did not approve, but he did acknowledge that 'these ladies are strenuously and conscientiously doing what they conceive to be their duty... We may learn, some of us, that we have underrated the strength and tenacity of determined womanhood'.[63]

By 1908 the WSPU was firmly established in Birmingham. The need for effective campaigning around the country became even more urgent as in April the former Chancellor of the Exchequer, Herbert Henry Asquith, succeeded Henry Campbell-

Bannerman to become Prime Minister. Asquith was unequivocal in his opposition to votes for women and his becoming PM would result in the WSPU employing ever more extreme tactics as he refused to change his mind. The progress that the militants felt they had made over the past twelve months was given in an overview of the national organisation in the April edition of *Votes for Women*: from February 1907 until February 1908 there were upwards of 5,000 meetings, 13 by-elections had been contested, many with reduced Liberal majorities, and 400 of their meetings had over 1,000 people in attendance. More ominously, however, it was stated that 130 women had been imprisoned. The ways in which people could help included becoming members, subscribing to the funds, circulating literature, organising meetings, giving time and services, carrying out missionary work, and generally becoming more involved with the movement.[64]

In February that year another deputation, 'The Women's Parliament', went to London, resulting in a number of arrests for attempting to enter the House of Commons. These included six Birmingham women – Ida Cunard, Mrs Wood, Laura Hemming, Marie Edwards, Mrs Aldis, and Edith Kerwood, all of whom received a six-week prison sentence in the second division, to be served in Holloway. The grim prison arrangements the women had to endure were described in *Votes for Women*: 'All the women sent to Holloway in connection with the attempt to reach the House of Commons are in the second division. They wear prison dress, eat prison food, are in their cells in solitary confinement for 23 hours out of 24, have no access to one another, are not allowed papers or letters or visits from their friends. Half an hour each day they have exercise, half an hour for chapel. During the day they are set to work to make mail bags or to darn. After 5pm they may, if they like, read one of the books in the prison library.'

A report provided by Elizabeth Redfern in early 1908, a shorthand writer at the county court and now the temporary WSPU organiser for Birmingham, stated that the group 'continues to make headway', as the organiser and members continued to work in the city and suburbs, and 'much has been done in arousing local sympathy and interest in the agitation for the enfranchisement of women'. Plans were being made for a reception to welcome back the six arrested women after completing their prison sentences and from this period fortnightly meetings would be held, 'of an interesting and educational character'. Letters of support from members were published, including from Ida Cunard and Edith Kerwood, who had completed their sentences. Cunard pleaded for members to 'rally around our beloved leaders, giving them first of all our undivided loyalty, and the Union unbounded enthusiasm, and the help that lies each in her individual power', while Kerwood urged members to 'have courage to do what is right, and never fear the consequences. Set principle above expediency, and never rest until you have gained your constitutional right – the Vote!'[65]

Towards the end of the year Birmingham welcomed a new organiser, Gladice Keevil. Well-educated, young and from the middle classes, Keevil had been a governess abroad and joined the WSPU when she returned. She had been part of the February deputation to Parliament and had also been arrested, becoming a WSPU organiser shortly after her release. She was then appointed to become Midlands organiser in September.[66] Following a successful demonstration at London's Hyde Park in June at which over 250,000 people were present, in July the Birmingham WSPU held 'a most successful meeting at Small Heath Park gates where hundreds of people collected and listened with great attention for over an hour and a half'. The meeting was chaired by Gladys Hazel, a teacher of English literature at King Edward's Girls Grammar School in Aston, while Dr Helena Jones, Medical Officer to Kings Norton Educational Board, spoke. They collected 9s and sold out of copies of *Votes for Women*. These early days of the organisation, with its new, young, confident and energetic local officers, meant that momentum was clearly now building. Meetings were held all throughout that summer, as well as the regular thrice-weekly ones, which resulted in 'much interest… and our audience are hoping that we shall be able to have a demonstration in September'.[67]

In the 15 October issue of *Votes for Women*, Gladice Keevil reported on what had happened when Asquith visited Birmingham the previous week to address the Classical Association in the Town Hall. Frequent protests and interruptions at meetings meant that 'the most elaborate precautions had been taken to exclude any possible Suffragette. Notwithstanding, we made our presence felt both inside and outside the Town Hall'. While some of the women sold newspapers and distributed handbills from outside, Keevil and Helena Jones managed to enter the hall. Towards the end of the meeting the two women approached Asquith: Keevil informed the reader that she 'advanced rapidly up the Hall during the applause' and demanded from the Prime Minister his plans for women's suffrage this session while she offered him a current copy of *Votes for Women*. They were able to leave the meeting without being arrested and Keevil's account demonstrates a sense of pride in this, that they were able to easily approach the Prime Minister, successfully attracting the attention of press and the outrage of witnesses. By the end of the month a permanent office, the walls papered in the WSPU colours of purple, green and white (matching curtains had been donated by wealthy fellow WSPU member Bertha Brewster), had been opened at 14 Ethel Street in the city centre, where evening 'At-Homes' were held on a Tuesday while afternoon meetings took place at the Edgbaston Assembly Rooms.[68]

Catherine Osler, President of the Birmingham Women's Suffrage Society and a prominent figure in the suffrage movement over many decades.

Millicent Garrett Fawcett, President of the National Union of Women's Suffrage Societies and leading national advocate of constitutional approaches to the suffrage campaign.

Emmeline Pankhurst with daughters Christabel and Sylvia (centre and right). The Pankhursts were the founders of the Women's Social and Political Union, and leading proponents of direct action as a campaigning tool.

28

Emmeline Pankhurst speaking at a public event, 1910.

OUTRAGES BY SUFFRAGETTES.

Just as Mr. Asquith's special train was leaving Birmingham for London at 10.25 last night, a stone was thrown fr m the barrier on the platform, and it smashed the window of the rear compartment, which, as it happened, was empty. For the escapade two women were arrested. In all eight Suffragettes were arrested.

Around Bingley Hall many exciting incidents occurred. Three women harangued the crowd from an upper window facing the front entrance of the hall. But the speeches, drowned in the jeers of the crowd, ceased, and there followed a fusillade of toy bombs on the cordon of police guarding the hall. These "bombs" were made of two pieces of cast iron with a small charge of fulminate between. They weighed about one and a half to two ounces, and might have done serious damage had they struck anyone. Happily, the feminine aim was too excited to be accurate.

The most serious scene, however, was when two of the Suffragettes ensconced themselves behind a chimney-stack in Cumberland-street, at the rear of the hall, and commenced tearing off slates from the roof and throwing them wildly among the crowd. The fire brigade was summoned, but the hose had little effect, and finally, when Mr. Asquith left, passing down Cambridge-street in order to avoid Broad-street, a large slate hit the top of his car. A detective was injured on the foot. Ultimately the police succeeded in scaling the roof by a back way and capturing the drenched Suffragettes, who were brought down a fire-escape to the street.

The Globe reports suffragette protests marking Prime Minister Asquith's visit to Bingley Hall in September 1909. 'Toy bombs' and roof slates were thrown by protesters.

Julia Varley, a trade unionist who worked with Cadburys' to organise their women workers. She was a member of both the WSPU and the BWSS during her career.

VOTES FOR WOMEN
EEP THE
RAL OUT.

Gladice Keevil came to Birmingham in 1908, shortly after this photograph was taken. Her organising experience helped grow the Birmingham branch of the WSPU.

Hilda Burkitt as a young woman. She was an indefatigable member of the Birmingham WSPU and active campaigner, being arrested for her actions numerous times.

MISS BURKETT.
MR ROBINSON
MR WHEELER
MISS SMITH B.A.
MISS REDFERN
MISS NELLIE KENNEY
MR BLAKEMAN WELCH
MR BLOXHAM
THE PRINCIPAL SPEAKERS.

Suffrage Campaigners, including Hilda Burkitt (top left), debate the issue at Aston Manor Parliament, 1908.

Wolverhampton WSPU member Emma Sproson chalking a pavement. Chalking to advertise meetings and publicise slogans was a popular activity for campaigners.

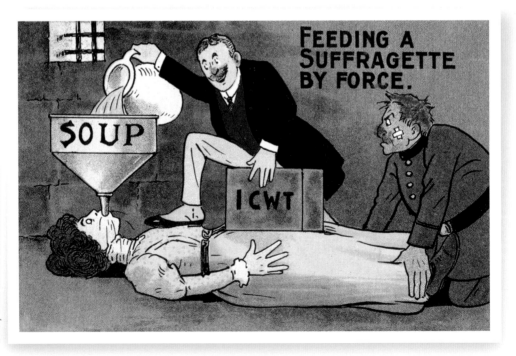

Forcible feeding of a hunger-striking suffragette in prison. The reality of forcible feeding was not much less brutal than this cartoon suggests.

Early photograph of Winson Green Gaol, 1908. This forbidding institution gained the dubious renown of being the first to enact forcible feeding on hunger-striking suffrage campaigners.

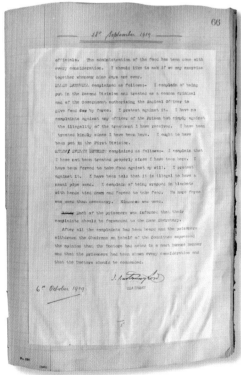

Forcible feeding in her own words: Hilda Burkitt's statement taken by the Winson Green visiting committee while she was imprisoned there in 1909.

The Common Cause, publication of the NUWSS, poking fun at some of those opposing women's suffrage, 1910.

This anti-suffrage cartoon is typical in its depiction of the suffragette speaker as an unappealing, unfeminine character, unconvincing to her audience.

Membership of suffrage societies was proudly celebrated: WSPU badge in the colours that would become indelibly associated with the movement; Birmingham Women's Suffrage Society banner in its red, white and green colours.

‘No vote – no census'. The intention of suffrage campaigners to evade the census or spoil their entries was widely known. *Birmingham Pictorial & Dart*, March 1911.

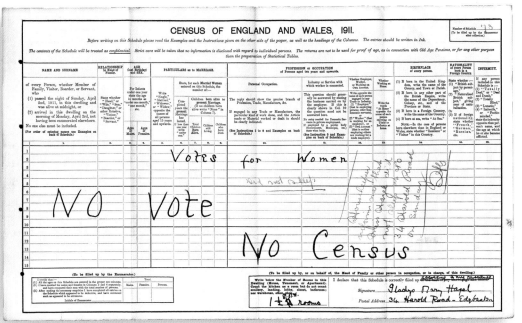

Gladys Hazel, resident in Harold Road, Edgbaston in 1911, was one of those who chose to spoil her entry, leaving census enumerators in no doubt about her position.

Female chain-makers listen to campaigner Mary Macarthur during the strike for a living wage, Cradley Heath 1910. Suffrage campaigners in the West Midlands targeted these organised and motivated groups of working-class women for their support.

The NUWSS Pilgrimage passes through Birmingham in 1913, advertising its peaceful approach, but one still captured in this police photograph.

During that same period outdoor meetings continued across the city, held, amongst other works, at the Carlyle & Dunlop Factory, Monument Road, Perry's Factory, Kynoch's Factory, the Institute in Northfield, Oozells Street Girls Club, and at the Physical Training College in Erdington, while 'a large number of working girls at Cadbury's wear the Votes for Women badge and it is the subject of animated discussion at the works'.[69] Badges cost a penny each. The organisation of women workers was evidently encouraged by the Cadburys. A branch of the National Federation of Women Workers had been set up at Bournville in 1907. Its popularity from the outset was clear and the *Bournville Works Magazine* reported that 200 women had joined immediately, with another 100 expected to join, 'the enthusiasm shown is very encouraging'.[70] Women's enfranchisement continued to be discussed on the pages of the *Bournville Works Magazine*. In 1908 a competition had been run which invited responses to the question, 'State what advantages, immediate and ultimate, you believe will be secured to the women and community generally of this district by the passing of a Bill to enfranchise women'. First prize went to Georgina McKenzie (second prize went to a male employee, Morris Yeomans). In her article, Georgina considered the benefits that having the vote would present to society, including prison reform, abolishment of sweated industries, and improved legal rights over a woman's children.[71] The following year Julia Varley, trade unionist and member of the Independent Labour Party, was invited to Birmingham by Edward Cadbury and George Shann to assist them in their regional organising work and she then led the branch of the National Federation of Women Workers. Julia was also a member of the WSPU and had been twice imprisoned in 1907 after her involvement with deputations to Parliament. Her involvement with the militant cause ended in 1912, however, when she left the WSPU and joined the BWSS.

Elizabeth Redfern, now honorary secretary for the branch, provided another review of 1908 to 'mark the strong foundation of the Women's Movement in Birmingham and district'. Since the formation of the Birmingham WSPU three large meetings had been held in the Town Hall, as well as innumerable indoor and outdoor meetings, all with great success. The report continued, 'as was only to be expected, the patient efforts of the local workers, the untiring zeal of the preceding organisers, the growth of the agitation generally, culminating in the midsummer demonstration, could not fail to make a lasting impression… The most has been made of every factor in the progress of the movement in the Midlands'. Through the setting up of a permanent central office and the establishment of gatherings, 'it is hoped that ere long Birmingham may rival London only in the importance of these At-Homes'. Of the members mentioned by name, Bertha

Ryland, daughter of BWSS member Alice Ryland, is singled out for special praise, for having 'worked with real devotion since Miss Keevil's advent'.[72] Bertha had also been a sometime subscriber to the BWSS, her name appearing alongside that of both of her parents in the annual reports for 1905-6, but she typified the new, younger generation of suffragist (she was born in 1882), part of the Birmingham liberal elite and involved in good causes but evidently frustrated with the slow pace of change. The WSPU offered her an alternative. Others mentioned include Gladys Hazel, the teacher from King Edward's Girls School who was in charge of the speakers' classes, and Hilda Burkitt, a 32-year-old member living in Sparkbrook at the time, who was tasked with advertising. These young, energetic and intelligent women were not rash, impatient girls but women who had been involved in the campaign for a number of years and with good reason. Many joined because they had witnessed first-hand the poverty that some women were forced to live in, in Birmingham and other cities in the country, while others felt their personal and professional ambitions were thwarted by merely by being a woman. All were dedicated and determined to go further than their predecessors and secure the vote for women.

'It is grand being a Suffragette!'

The following year, in April 1909, possibly influenced by the WSPU, the NUWSS began to publish its own newspaper, *The Common Cause*. Like *Votes for Women* it included regional updates, including one from the Birmingham Society, which had recently opened a new office at 10 Easy Row, not far from the WSPU base. The sense of diligent activity was palpable: 'it is in an excellent central position, so that our signboard is seen by hundreds of people passing to business or to do their shopping every day'. A stock of pamphlets was available for purchase, including the WSPU's paper *Votes for Women*, and there was a small lending library. A meeting was planned for every Wednesday morning which was to include a speech and, if time, 'end with a sharp practice debate to encourage new speakers'. Women were being offered education and training in order to argue confidently for their right to vote. For the summer months 'cycle rides to neighbouring villages for outdoor work' were planned. A by-election in South-West Warwickshire in May presented the opportunity for members of the BWSS to experience canvassing at the polling booths: 'for most it was an entirely new experience; to all it was interesting, though some did not find it altogether pleasant', and there were reports of booing and stone throwing by those hostile to the cause.[73] By the middle of the year the Society reported an increase in subscribing members from 220 to 531 and an income increase from £106 to £569, although the Berkswell branch had been dissolved after the leading members defected to the WSPU. Despite advances in the campaign, there were still women impatient with the constitutional focus. There were other reports of women being publicly heckled, and, as in 1907, university students were the culprits: at a meeting held at Monument Road 'unfortunately the students had come to hear of this, so proceedings were rather disorderly'.[74]

The WSPU had the same problem. In May at a meeting at which Emmeline Pethick Lawrence spoke, a petition was presented to the women, stating that the admission price for men at the meetings should be reduced so that working men might attend in greater numbers. However, Gladice Keevil responded that the prices were deliberately raised in order to keep out the male university students.[75] Despite fears around heckling, the BWSS also now began to hold meetings at the Bull Ring, although they remarked that it was 'a place we had always been warned against'. However, it was so successful that they decided to hold regular meetings there. They also held meetings at factories across the city including Elkington's (although, unsuccessfully, as they were moved on by the police because of a bad pitch) and at the BSA works, where the directors allowed them to speak inside the private grounds from a platform erected by the men.[76]

During this period, the WSPU continued to go from strength to strength and a spike in membership was reported in the spring of 1909: 50 new members joined in the first week of March 1909. This was probably due to an appearance by Christabel Pankhurst at a meeting at the Town Hall the month before, where she 'received an ovation the like of which no woman has ever experienced in Birmingham', stated the report in *Votes for Women*, as modest as ever.[77] The *Birmingham Weekly Mercury* reported the event on 27 February. In the build-up to the meeting there was a procession through the city on a wagon, decorated in the WSPU colours, on which were seated four suffragettes dressed in replica prison costumes complete with arrows. They were made by police to remove their banners but then returned with another banner with the word 'Christabel' on it. The newspaper then described Christabel's speech, undaunted by her recent prison experience 'her arms constantly extended in suffrage-seeking appeal, and her eyes flashing with righteous indignation'. The article also described Gladice Keevil, who had chaired the meeting, albeit in somewhat patronising terms, who 'with chin upthrust and fluttering hands, made a charming picture of earnest and at the same time attractive femininity'.

It was also in March 1909 that the Birmingham WSPU office was pleased to announce the formation of a local branch of the Men's League for Women's Suffrage, which had been established in London around 1907, and was organised in Birmingham by A. W. Evans of 332 Moseley Road. The appeal of the WSPU for younger women and girls and working-class women was also evident in a letter sent to *Votes for Women*. May Davis, a schoolgirl at King Edward's School, Camp Hill, wrote about an 'At-Home' meeting that had been given by a school friend, Sylvia Hill, at her home in Northfield. A room in the house was 'decorated in the colours, and we were presented with bouquets of purple, white and green… I think the meeting was a success, because when it was over there were only three who did not agree with the Suffragettes. It is grand being a Suffragette, because we schoolgirls are beginning to see the seriousness of the movement and the necessity of having a vote, as a power for protection of our interests when we are older'.[78] Interestingly, in the 19 March branch update, there is mention of Mrs Ryland, 'our president'. This must be Alice Ryland, the mother of Bertha. Alice's position as an executive committee member of the BWSS at the same time demonstrates that, despite differences in approach and tactics, there were cases of overlapping memberships between the two organisations.

Gladice Keevil also reported in March that 'on Thursday last I addressed the girl workers in a rag factory in Birmingham. It was interesting to see the change in attitude after I had made clear our reasons for wanting the vote. "Promise to come again" they said, and I gladly promised'.[79] In addition to work being done in affluent areas of the city such as Edgbaston, there were also concerted efforts taking place in industrial working-class areas such as Saltley and Small Heath, led by Hilda Burkitt: 'this district has progressed almost more rapidly than any other in Birmingham, though I think Bournville under the captaincy of Mrs Edwards still stands first': Marie Edwards was one of the first Birmingham WSPU members to be imprisoned for protesting, sent to Holloway Gaol after being arrested during a deputation to Parliament in 1908.[80] The following month a meeting in Small Heath attracted a crowd of around 300, suggesting that working-class and industrial areas of the city were keen to hear the women's point of view. On 11 June Hilda reported that 'in spite of the inclement weather the public flock to our open-air meetings, and are waiting for us when we arrive, greeting us with "Here they come; three cheers for the Suffragettes"'. While the women could expect to be heckled at meetings, there were also plenty offers of support, often from men. Hilda described how 'one evening I happened to be quite alone. I held a short meeting and sold papers, one man saying 'I'll buy one,' 'cause I admire your pluck in standing up there all alone, Miss'.[81]

There were more arrests in the summer of 1909, after a deputation to London (none of the women arrested were Birmingham WSPU members), and a rousing call to action by Mrs Pankhurst was published in *Votes for Women*. The seriousness of what was at stake for the women was now clear and the potential dangers carried by choosing militancy were acknowledged: 'We are not crushed, and our organised Movement is not crushed by the violence shown towards us… We gladly offer both our life and our freedom in order that the women of the present and the future may live and may be free… And from the very day of our arrest this Movement will date an accession of energy, a renewal of determination, and an accretion of power… Women! Comrades! Dear Fellow-workers! I charge you, love this Movement, work for it, live for it. Let no thought of your own comfort and happiness hinder you from rendering it your whole service. Give it your thought, your time, your all. It is worth everything that you can give. It is the greatest cause in the world. Nothing in life is so important as the redemption of women from the yoke of the subjection, which has meant for centuries the degradation of the whole human race'. Tactics encouraged by Pankhurst included increasing the circulation of *Votes for Women*, contributing to the Campaign Fund, and learning how to speak in public: 'if you cannot speak, you can learn. No habit of ease or luxury must keep you now from throwing yourself into the work'.[82] The importance for women across both militant and constitutional sides in finding their own voice was central to the campaign, as was developing the strength and confidence to deal with hecklers and hostile crowds.

Meetings continued in Birmingham over the summer, increasing in number as they approached September and the planned visit by Prime Minister Asquith to the city to address a meeting of Liberals. Momentum was gathering and on 9 July Gladice Keevil wrote in *Votes for Women*, 'in all new places we now find the crowd waiting for us. At one meeting several people suggested that the Suffragettes were harming their cause, but no-one could put forward any better methods'. Throughout the month, local branch updates conjure up a picture of vibrant suffrage activity in the city: new Sunday meetings now took place at Cannon Hill Park, on Edgbaston Road and Russell Road, 'where people congregate on their way to the park'. 'The colours have been flying in the town during the greater part of the week, several shopkeepers having offered to display flags themselves. In the principal street of Birmingham, New Street, festoons of purple, white and green, have been hanging, and on Degree day at the new University three cheers were given for Votes for Women and Mrs Pankhurst'; presumably not by those who had heckled at the Town Hall meeting the previous year.[83] Birmingham's important position within the wider movement was clearly asserted by Keevil who remarked that 'as Birmingham is becoming the second largest city in the Empire it is most important that it should be thoroughly alive to our movement'.[84] Meetings held during the first fortnight of September included a huge range of locations across the city: Brooke's Factory on Livery Street, Holloway Head, Marshall Street, Floodgate Street, River Street, the Bull Ring, Dunlop's Factory in

Aston, Lea Bank Road, Wheeleys Lane, Ansell's Brewery, Jarret & Rainsford's Factory, Midlands Vinegar Co., Station Works in Saltley, Soho Road, Washwood Heath, Perry's at Lancaster Gate, Barton's Arms, Kynoch's Works, Iron Foundry on Alum Rock Road, Stratford Place, Camp Hill, Monument Road and Carriage Works.

Most elements of the mainstream press did not view the activities of the WSPU with equal enthusiasm, however. On 17 September *The Birmingham Owl* published an article titled 'Disappointed Suffragettes & Others'. Here they harshly proclaimed that 'the suffragette has no sense of propriety. She is rampant, violent, vulgar, and in most cases, and last but not least, unattractive. She is not beyond hawking the paper *"Votes for Women"* in the principal streets of Birmingham, but her winning smile does not increase the sale'. The writer then clarified the two different sides of the campaign: 'It does not appear to be generally understood that there is a distinction between the suffragette and the suffragist. The suffragette is the girl or woman of the militant order, who allows herself to be chained to railings, assaults the police, causes obstruction, endeavours to force an entrance into the House of Commons, worries the PM and other members of Parliament, pays fines or goes to gaol. The suffragist is the lady who is not rampant, but who endeavours to attain the desired end by quiet and constitutional means; by the holding of meetings, organisation carried on in a lady-like manner, representations to MPs made in a lady-like manner.'

The Bingley Hall incident

On 24 September 1909 *Votes for Women* published an eyewitness account of Prime Minister Asquith's recent appearance at Bingley Hall: 'At last Birmingham has been awakened to the fact that women are in deadly earnest in their demand for political freedom... The women made one of the most successful and effective protests that have ever been made.' Records held in the West Midlands Police Museum show that the police were prepared for disruption, given the WSPU track record of interrupting political meetings, and instructions were given that 'all tickets are marked not to admit a lady except certain special tickets'.[85] A total of 59 sergeants, 495 constables on foot and 20 on horseback were on duty in the city that evening, including one sergeant and 10 constables standing outside the Midland Institute where there was to be a BWSS meeting. Naturally, members of the WSPU tried to gain entry to the hall but were prevented from doing so by the heavy police presence. The records also show that the police were 'instructed to deal carefully with women and avoid using violence which is not necessary' but also that each person entering should be carefully scrutinised in case any women attempted to gain admission while dressed as men. Although no WSPU women were able to enter the hall, there were 15 interruptions to the meeting by male sympathisers who were ejected, some brutally.

If they could not enter the meeting then the WSPU were not going to miss the opportunity to cause disruption in other ways. Two of the women, Mary Leigh and Charlotte Marsh, members from London sent up for the demonstration, climbed onto the roof of a timber merchant's in nearby Cambridge Street and threw roof slates at Asquith's car: 'Their plans were carefully laid; in the streets both in front and at the back of Bingley Hall Suffragettes had been lodging for several days, and by nine o'clock on Friday morning there were upwards of a score of them safely stowed away there… Suddenly there was a sound of splintering glass, and a voice was heard denouncing the Government. Two windows of the outer office of Bingley Hall had been broken by the women in the house opposite. Literally dozens of policemen rushed into the house, tumbling over each other in their eagerness, and dragging the two women out, they threw them into the street, where they were immediately arrested… Two women had succeeded in climbing on to a neighbouring roof, from which, with the help of axes, they managed to dislodge some slates, which they flung on to the roof of the hall, and on to Mr Asquith's motor-car.'[86] Outside the hall six other women made repeated attempts to break through the barriers; according to reports, one of the women was seen flourishing a hammer.

As Asquith went to leave the meeting the description in the newspapers begins to sound farcical: Marsh and Leigh were threatened with the fire hose, although it was said that the pressure was insufficient for the stream of water to reach them. The women cried 'Do what you like! We want votes for members of Parliament. Do your worst', followed by 'No Surrender' and 'Liberty or death'.[87] The eyewitness continued: 'How is it that though the Prime Minister has all the protection that money and power can bring, still the women's voice is always heard? It is brute force pitted against spirit – spirit which is daunted by nothing – risk of injury, loss of liberty, starvation, even death itself if necessary. Such a force can never be defeated.'[88] Two more women, Hilda Burkitt and Ellen Barnwell (who was also from Birmingham), threw a piece of metal through one of the train carriage windows while shouting 'Votes for Women!' as it left the station.[89] All ten women were arrested. Burkitt and Barnwell were sentenced to one month in the second division and taken to Winson Green Gaol, where all of the women commenced a hunger strike.

In 1908 Hilda Burkitt had appeared in the *Birmingham Weekly Mercury*, participating in a debate about women's suffrage held at the Aston Manor Parliament, a borough constituency that had been created from North Warwickshire in 1885. Hilda's comments during that debate would prove to be especially pertinent, given her prison experiences from 1909 to 1914: she remarked that women had quite as much stamina as men, and believed they were capable of bearing more pain.[90] Hilda had already been in trouble with the police in the months before the Bingley Hall demonstration and had been arrested three times. In April she had been in court in Wolverhampton where she was charged with obstructing the police during a political meeting. The judge dismissed her by telling her to go back to Birmingham and not to bother them again. And in August she was in court in Hull, along with a number of other suffragettes, this time for demonstrating outside the city's Assembly Rooms.[91]

Votes for Women on 24 September also included an article by Mrs Pankhurst on militancy. In 'Is it right? Is it wrong?' she argued: 'It must be remembered that this war of freedom was begun when women had deliberately arrived at the conclusion that after forty unavailing years, the uses of argument and persuasion were at an end.' She continued: 'Women, in direct opposition to their instinct, tradition, and normal character, have thus been forced into a revolution in defence of their rights and liberties, and for this the Government is responsible, and not the women.' In Pankhurst's opinion, the methods were beginning to work: 'We are pressing the Government hard, driving them by our militant action and by the passive resistance of the hunger strike, into a corner from which there is no outlet except by giving votes to women. They, too, are pressing us hard, driving us into a corner by their relentless repressions, from which there is no outlet except by the adoption of methods which we hate. The question is, Who will yield first? Not the women, because they are fighting for a fundamentally sacred cause which they dare not betray by abandoning the fight… This is a revolution. This is a war. But it is a revolution forced upon us. It is a war which we are called upon to wage in the name of liberty and justice. Let the heart of every woman in the movement be the heart of a hero and a warrior, then shall we fight unflinchingly to the very end, and shall forget the strain and the stress in the joy of the battle, which is bound to end in victory for the right.' Unbeknown to Pankhurst, this 'war' would continue for a number of years before any satisfactory outcome was achieved. It was also about to take a dramatic turn.

The protest was not restricted only to the militants. An article in the 16 September issue of *The Common Cause* titled 'Indignation meeting in Birmingham' described plans the BWSS had for a gathering to take place at the Midland Institute the night Asquith came to the city. Those present would include Mary Sturge (medical practitioner, suffragist and niece of Eliza Sturge), Ethel Snowden (one of the NUWSS national speakers), Eva

Gore-Booth (the suffragist from Manchester who had visited the Cradley Heath chain makers in 1904), and other women who included staff from the University, those involved with the Temperance movement, clerks, civil servants, factory workers, and women workers from other industries. Given the expected attendance it was unsurprising that the BWSS was of the opinion that 'such a meeting as this should be an excellent and weighty protest against the present extraordinary condition of things in which, bit by bit, women are being deprived of all constitutional means of making their claim heard by members of the Government. They have been excluded from all Ministers' meetings, and they cannot even have any questions asked for them'.

Unlike Campbell-Bannerman, Asquith was far more reluctant to meet with suffragist deputations or to even listen to their arguments. Later in the same issue of *The Common Cause* it was revealed that some members of the Women's Liberal Association were going to be permitted entry, after much protesting, and that this included Catherine Osler. It was asserted that 'we feel most strongly that any woman who is prepared to undertake not to interrupt should be allowed to come in', but there was an acknowledgement of the difficulties for Liberal women, long-serving and loyal party supporters, that the wider exclusion from the meeting presented. In a letter published in *The Common Cause* on 30 September, Miss L. R. Taylor, BWSS member and, until March 1909, branch secretary, defended accusations of betrayal levelled at the Liberal women who attended, stating 'they were asked to sign names in a book, and one, the President [Osler], refused to do that, saying she would not do one single thing that a man had not been asked to do'. The women who were present also refused to stand or applaud Asquith during the meeting.

The week after the incident *The Common Cause* had coverage of the indignation meeting on the front page. The hall at the Midland Institute, which could hold 1,000 people, was completely packed by women from a wide range of backgrounds and classes, 'the wealthy women of Edgbaston came in their carriages, there were young girls from the factories who had been brought to take an interest in the movement by the persuasive arguments of Miss Cooper [Selina, a suffragist from Nelson, Lancashire]... nurses, academics, Temperance workers, clerks, medical women, charwomen'. As she had been allowed into the meeting at Bingley Hall, Catherine Osler had sent a letter of apology in which she wrote: 'Women citizens had undoubted reason to feel insulted and injured when denied the right of listening to the exposition by the Prime Minister of proposals which affected them equally with men, and on which they were refused the expression of an opinion through the vote. The injury and insult would be most keenly felt by those who like herself strongly condemned disorder and violence as a means of public agitation.' Despite the huge numbers present, the Society was yet again aware that its meeting would garner far less publicity than the actions of the WSPU, and Ethel Snowden observed that 'the disturbances outside would get several columns, while this splendid meeting would not get more than a few lines'.[92]

The impact of the militant action undertaken outside Bingley Hall was considered by the constitutional suffragists the following week in an article in *The Common Cause*, alarmingly titled 'Hooliganism in Birmingham'.[93] The journal observed that 'matters are becoming somewhat serious in Birmingham. The crowd, never over friendly in the birthplace of Austen Chamberlain, has now come to consider any woman fair game… It may be that Birmingham is particularly retrograde… There is no doubt that the action at Bingley Hall has meant a great setback for the cause in Birmingham, and that has made our work increasingly difficult. If it is also to mean that innocent women are to be insulted at will, we shall have additional reason to regret it'.[94] One particularly unpleasant incident had involved Miss L. R. Taylor. On leaving the BWSS office on Easy Row, Taylor was accosted by a crowd in the street. Someone in the crowd called out that she was a suffragette and began to jostle her, pulling at her coat, although she managed to escape unharmed. However, a far more serious incident was also reported. A woman had been set upon on Bridge Street by a group who tried to tear off all her clothes before other members of the public intervened. While the reaction of some members of the public towards the women became more unsympathetic and even threatening, the events at Bingley Hall were about to thrust the militant movement into a far more dangerous phase of the campaign.

Forcible feeding

The treatment of the ten Bingley Hall protesters imprisoned in Winson Green Gaol was revealed at the end of the month. Hunger-striking as a tactic had only just been adopted, influenced by Russian political prisoners demonstrating against the oppressive tsarist regime, and instigated by Marion Wallace-Dunlop, a member of the WSPU who had been imprisoned in Holloway in July that year. She had protested against her treatment as a common criminal within the prison system and demanded that she be moved from the second division to the first in recognition for her conviction for a political offence.[95] Dunlop had been released from custody before she became too seriously ill.

Letters between the Chief Constable of the Birmingham Police, the Governor of Winson Green and the Home Office reveal how the treatment of the prisoners was planned. In a letter dated 18 September, Chief Constable Rafter commented that if the hunger-striking women were 'dealt with firmly now' and not released but forcibly fed, 'it would have a very high moral effect in putting an end to the nuisance here and perhaps elsewhere'. He also described a previous case of a male prisoner at Winson Green who was forcibly fed and then began taking food of his own accord. This was presented as evidence that the prison was capable of carrying out the treatment and that it worked. The Constable's main concern was that the women were not to be treated leniently and would be made to complete their sentences.[96] A memo from the Governor of Winson Green and the Medical Officer, Dr Helby, to the Home Office dated 20 September referred to Burkitt and Barnwell, 'neither of robust appearance', and that they were of the opinion that 'prolonged abstinence from food will be injurious to their health'. The response from the Home Office was 'to feed artificially'. The Governor was also instructed to call in medical expert advice and consult as to the best means of administering the treatment, 'i.e. by mouth or nostril; also as to the best means to avoid struggle, involving danger or unnecessary pain' and also to consider if using a canvas suit (straitjacket) was the best method to employ.[97] After discovering this, the WSPU attempted to sue the Government on behalf of two of the prisoners, Charlotte Marsh and Mary Leigh, both of whom had received the longest sentences.

The issue quickly became a national one as questions were asked in Parliament, most persistently by Keir Hardie, Labour Party leader. In his private correspondence to the Home Office, Dr William Cassels, another of the Winson Green medical officers, disregarded assertions that forcible feeding produced intense vomiting. On one occasion, he argued that although Mary Leigh had vomited for hours after being fed, this was probably self-induced.[98] The debate was then played out on the pages of the newspapers between doctors of differing opinions. In one of the local journals the reaction was less than sympathetic. *The Birmingham Pictorial & Dart* wrote proudly in an article that appeared on the front page: 'Birmingham has once more led the way – this time, in the treatment of the Suffragettes. In other parts of the country, and particularly in London, the prison authorities have been defeated by these starving tactics and have liberated the women before their time expired. Now, Birmingham has created a precedent and, doubtless, others will follow. On Monday and Tuesday afternoon, Mr Keir Hardie and Mr Snowden[99] both lashed themselves into a fury over it, but Mr Masterman[100] answered laconically that the authorities were quite justified in their treatment, and that the prisoners were doing well under it. After all, when one remembers that these women made serious attempts on the life of the PM by throwing roof slates and other dangerous missiles, one not need be too nice in the method of punishment. It is not a case of dealing with women of gentle and refined natures, but with female hooligans of pronounced homicidal tendencies. They are criminals of a particularly vicious sort, and well deserve the stomach pump and other things.'[101]

After petitioning the Government, statements were then taken from each of the women by the chairman of a committee formed by the Government. Hilda Burkitt's statement was given as follows: 'I complain that I have not been treated properly since I have been here. I have been forced to take food against my will. I protest against it. I have been told that it is illegal to have a nasal pipe used. I complain of being wrapped in blankets with hands tied down and forced to take food. No more force was used than necessary. Kindness was used.' Hilda's statement is a peculiar and unsettling mix of protestation and commendation. It is difficult to ascertain how much of the statement is an accurate portrayal of Hilda's feelings and how much was coerced by the interviewer, and her remark that she was treated kindly seems the most challenging part of the statement for modern readers to believe. The minute book also records that 'the doctors had acted in a most humane manner and that the prisoners had been shown every consideration and that the doctors should be commended'.[102] While the women were incarcerated, demonstrations took place every evening at the Bull Ring, where speeches were delivered from a wagonette, 'and speakers then ask the crowd to follow them to Winson Green to give the prisoners a rousing cheer'. Funds were also raised to pay a band to play outside the prison. The protests, led by Bertha Ryland, 'met with a great deal of sympathy, especially among the working women'.[103]

Protests did not only take place outside Winson Green, however. Some women turned up at the home of the prison's deputy medical officer, William Cassels, who lived at 294 Soho Road in Handsworth. Cassels was besieged by WSPU members, who stuck propaganda posters all over his windows, threw stones and held sandwich parades outside the house with slogans like 'Who tortures women in prison!'[104] Protests continued up to November as two of the prisoners, Mary Leigh and Charlotte Marsh, were still being held. An attempt to hold a meeting in Victoria Square on the evening of 24 November ended in multiple arrests. These included Gladys Hazel and Nellie Hall, a local 16-year-old member of the WSPU, both charged with being disorderly and causing an obstruction. *Votes for Women* noted that 'the doctors are still compelled to have police protection night and day... It is understood that forty police have been drafted into Birmingham, and that another forty are expected very soon. On Saturday afternoon parties went out into the different parts of the town, chalking protests against Miss Marsh's torture at Winson Green, and demanding her release'. A famous showman, Mr Waller Jeffs, was going to be 'showing pictures of various aspects of the movement with Miss Marsh's photograph on his bioscope at the Curzon Hall'.[105] Marsh was eventually released on 15 December.

Hilda Burkitt was released on 16 October and taken to her home at 81 Grantham Road, Sparkbrook. The account of her prison experience that was published in the 22 October issue of *Votes for Women* offers a stark contrast to her official statement, possibly giving a more accurate version of events but one that may also have been dramatized by the newspaper for full effect. Nonetheless, it is an extremely harrowing account of what the invasive treatment would have been like. Hilda had gone on hunger strikes, lasting for 81 hours, 96 hours and 24 hours, respectively: 'On arriving at the prison she refused to take off her clothes or to take any food… She stated to him [doctor] that she wished to send a petition to the Home Secretary to be placed in the first division.' On Tuesday afternoon 'she was taken into the hospital kitchen. There were two doctors, four wardresses, and matron. They forced her to sit in a chair and tried to wrap a blanket around her. A struggle then ensued, but she was eventually overpowered by wardresses and held in the chair. She said: "I will not take food! I refuse! I will not swallow!" Her lips were forced open and food poured from a feeding cup through the crevices of her teeth, which remained closed. She did not swallow any, and after half an hour they gave it up. She was now fearfully weak. The prison doctor then said: "Well, illegal or not, I'm going to use it". The nasal tube was then forced up, but she coughed it back twice. She was supported back to her cell and put in bed by the wardresses. Miss Burkitt then said: "This, I think, will kill me sooner than starving; I can't stand much more of it, but I am proud you have not beaten me yet"'. The next attempt involved the stomach pump, 'then more food was forced down by one doctor and two wardresses in a new way. The doctor stood behind, pushed the patient into a reclining position, caught hold of her throat, then forced the feeding cup into her mouth… She had very great pain at night… She only slept four nights out of the whole month'.[106] In her petition to be classed as a political prisoner, Hilda wrote 'I am ready to lay down my life, to bring about the freedom of my Sex'.[107] There is a sense of inevitability in Hilda's statement, an acceptance that this was to be her life as a militant suffragette, fully devoted to the cause.

On the front page of the 7 October edition of *The Common Cause*, the issue of forcible feeding was discussed and a number of questions were raised. Although militancy was not condoned, members of the NUWSS were outraged that women could be treated in such a violent manner. They demanded to know who was carrying out the treatment in the prison and how and why the decision to begin the forcible feeding of women hunger-strikers had been made. There were also questions around why the women were not given access to their own medical advisers, and it seemed 'to the outside public there cannot be but something sinister in the total exclusion of any independent testimony. All the reports we have are given by those who have a system to defend'. In that same issue, in an article titled 'Liberal Secessionalists', readers learned of Catherine Osler's resignation from the Women's Liberal Association, along with three other Birmingham women, Gertrude Southall, Elsie Yoxall and Edith Reid, Catherine's sister. This was a major step for Catherine and her colleagues to undertake but the women had evidently lost patience with Liberal politicians. In a clear signal of the priority for them of women's suffrage over party loyalty (and possibly also in dismay at the decision to forcibly feed women prisoners), the women commented, 'we have long felt our divided duty to be a burden difficult to bear… continued disappointment has forced us to resolve that we can take no further part in actively working for those who deny women the rights of citizenship'.

Catherine's resignation was also reported in the local press, where some sympathy with her position was expressed. An article titled 'Mrs Osler and Women's Suffrage', published in *The Birmingham Pictorial & Dart* on 8 October, observed: 'Few among us sympathise with the methods of the militant Suffragettes, but the secession of Mrs Osler from the Birmingham Liberal Association directs attention to the fact that there is something in the claim of justification advanced by these women. Mrs Osler has been working for the cause of the enfranchisement of women for thirty years, but her methods have always been of the constitutional order. She has, in short, deluded herself into the belief that the Liberal Party had a feeling of gratitude towards the women who, like herself, have devoted most of their leisure to politics. It has taken her a quarter of a century to realise that she has made a mistake, but Mrs Osler, and the ladies who have resigned with her, have made a protest which is at once dignified and effective… Her services to the Liberal Party in Birmingham have been invaluable, and if other women of her type act in a similar manner, then the "Votes for Women" cause will advance more rapidly than the hooligan-brand of advocacy can ever hope to push it forward.'

After recovering from her prison ordeal, Hilda Burkitt continued with militant activism but she was often met with fierce opposition from members of the public. A month after her release she appeared in the newspapers again: on 26 November *The Mercury* covered a campaign meeting that had taken place at Walsall, organised by the

Birmingham WSPU office. Hilda tried to speak at the meeting but 'was pushed off a chair on which she was standing, and she was also pelted with rotten apples and other similar missiles'. The women were forced to stop the meeting. At the end of 1909 it was announced that Gladice Keevil was giving up organising work in and around Birmingham to go to Exeter. It was not uncommon for the WSPU to move organisers on from their posts after a period of 12 months or so, and indeed, it was widely accepted that the 'post as a WSPU organiser involved a demanding and itinerant life away from home'.[108] Keevil expressed her 'deep thanks to the many members, far too numerous to mention by name, who have rallied around and so made it possible for the Birmingham centre to become such a strong one during the last thirteen months'.[109] The intense efforts made by both militant and constitutional workers over the short period of 1906 to 1909 meant that Birmingham was now unequivocally established as a stronghold of the movement, with both arms of the campaign full of vibrant, energetic and determined women, dedicated to winning women the right to vote. However, the Liberal Government, led by Asquith, would not give in easily and the next few years would see some shocking incidents take place in Birmingham.

Campaigning, census evasion and increased militancy: 1910 – 1912

'Repression cannot break the spirit of liberty'

Christabel Pankhurst, 1912

The campaign continues

Newspaper coverage of the events at Bingley Hall confirmed the opinion held by members of the Birmingham Women's Suffrage Society that they were being deliberately ignored by the newspapers. They had even observed in their annual report for the previous year that 'the attitude of the Press is still unsatisfactory. Reports are generally totally inadequate, though there is some endeavour to be fair. There is still a conspiracy of silence against the educational work of all the Societies'.[110] Never ones to be deterred, however, the BWSS was able to extend and develop its activities in 1910, aided by Asquith's decision in late 1909 to announce a General Election. This was to take place in January, after the House of Lords rejected Chancellor of the Exchequer, David Lloyd George's "Peoples' Budget", which would have significantly increased taxes on the wealthy. The election allowed suffragist campaigners to push for women's votes, writing to parliamentary candidates asking for their support, accompanied by an electors' petition which urged the removal of the sex disability and asked candidates three questions: 'Will you, in your election address, declare yourself to be a supporter of the enfranchisement of women? Will you do everything in your power to press its urgency upon your party leaders? Will you oppose the enactment of any measure for extending the franchise to men which does not include women?'[111] The demands of the national campaign continued to emphasise 'votes for women on the same terms as it is or may be granted to men', along with refusal of party affiliation, stating: 'We belong to no party and support no party as such. We support the best friends to women's enfranchisement in all parties. Our method is by orderly propaganda and public discussion to put the question before the electors, that they may induce Members of Parliament to press it forward.'[112]

The BWSS quickly and effectively mobilised across the city, setting up committee rooms, each one a centre for the distribution of literature and a venue for holding meetings. The update provided by the branch for *The Common Cause* on 6 January informed readers that Catherine Osler's daughter-in-law, Elsie, frequently completed 12-hour shifts in Saltley, from where she was running the East Birmingham campaign, and had been organising outdoor meetings on Alum Rock Road outside the Metropolitan Carriage Works, where on one occasion 'the audience announced themselves as converted, and the signing of the petition was begun'.[113] Other committee rooms were set up in Gooch Street to cover South Birmingham, Coventry Road in Bordesley, High Street, Smethwick and Soho Road in Handsworth. Another one of the members, Miss Kirby, who worked in the North Birmingham area, was reported to be carrying out 'splendid plodding, dull work', and apparently spent every evening from 7pm until 9.30pm with three other members making house-to-house visits with a voters' petition, handing out leaflets and encouraging people to support the cause.[114] Miss L. R. Taylor, the former BWSS secretary, spoke so much that she lost her voice. Around 250 outdoor meetings were held during the campaign, taking place during dinner hours outside factory gates and on street corners, including at the Bull Ring. Other favoured places for setting up pitches included near the Free Library in Bordesley, Moseley Road and Soho Road. In the week before election day in Birmingham on 15 January, approximately 12 to 15 meetings were being held across the city every day, 'the crowds are splendid, varying from a hundred to over a thousand. They are almost invariably attentive and sympathetic, and ask intelligent questions'.[115]

An account of polling day was given by the BWSS in the following week's edition of *The Common Cause*: 'a strenuous week ended with a still more strenuous day, but, thank goodness, it is over'. Bad weather had curtailed some of the outdoor meetings but around 50 were held, and 91 of the 120 districts were staffed with about 140 members working. The BWSS reported later that the petition 'when finished, was a sad sight of wet paper and blurred pencil marks', but 7,250 signatures had been successfully collected.[116] The reaction to the women was generally good, however; it was evident that the women had potentially changed opinions and, at the very least, had made people think about the issue. Comments from attending police officers were complimentary and one voter was reported to have said, 'I never believed in women's suffrage, but it's enough to convert me to see you ladies here'. The extent of their efforts and obvious dedication to the cause was clearly worthy of admiration by sceptical members of the public. It was also observed by the *Evening Despatch* that 'the militant Suffragists were conspicuous in their absence', and this arguably allowed the BWSS to further establish support for the constitutional cause: 'Our colours (red, white, green) are now well-known in Birmingham. Small boys tore the label off our car, but the gaily flying flags were enough to send the cry of "Votes for Women" all down the streets.'[117] The *Birmingham Daily Gazette* reported on 17 January that election day 'was practically free from incidents… the members of the Birmingham and Midlands Women's Suffrage Society did painstaking duty outside the various polling stations, but they were a passive army, the only object being to secure signatures to a petition in favour of the extension of the Parliamentary franchise'. It was later observed in their report for the year that two things had become apparent to BWSS members whilst out campaigning: 'one was the almost universal dislike of militant tactics, the other was the almost equally universal opinion that women householders should have votes, but that wives should not'.[118]

Despite these successes, they were still given far less attention in the press. Indeed, Catherine Osler recalled a journalist asking her if her organisation was going to do anything extraordinary, for if not then he was too busy to stay. Her solution given in the BWSS annual report was 'to do everything in our power to increase the circulation of our own press, *The Common Cause*, so that we may have a full and truthful account every week of the work that is being done all over the country'. However, the report also made the following point that 'our steady educational work is not sensational enough to supply striking headlines and nothing else is of use unless backed up by power and influence'.[119] The difficulties that some women had faced while out campaigning were also acknowledged. In the report from the city on 3 February, it was observed that 'the work, owing to the Chamberlain influence, must be particularly hard and uphill'. The National Women's Anti-Suffrage League, established in 1908 and amalgamated with the Men's League in 1910 to form the National League for Opposing Women's Suffrage, had successfully secured the support of Austen Chamberlain who, along with his father Joseph, held the now arguably old-fashioned opinion that separate spheres for men and women should be protected. Austen's sister, Beatrice, was also a member of the League.

The image on the front cover of the 3 February issue of *The Common Cause* epitomised the types of comments women across the country faced: 'Some Types of Electors' included cartoons of men alongside quotes such as 'women haven't sufficient strength of character', 'woman's place is the home', and 'go home and learn your manners'. Despite these challenges, BWSS member Miss Gardner wrote of the campaign: 'Polling-booth work is disagreeable in the most favourable conditions, but the more I see of it the more I am convinced that it is well worth doing, not for the signatures obtained, but for the moral effect on the voters.' In the end, the election resulted in a hung parliament with the Conservatives and their Liberal Unionist allies receiving the most votes. However, the Liberal Party secured a higher number of seats, returning two more MPs, and so the anti-suffragist Asquith was able to form a Government with the aid of the Irish Parliamentary Party, led by John Redmond.

Nevertheless, the BWSS took positives from the campaign and continued to fight. Women involved in the constitutional campaign were aware that, based on their previous experience, progress would not come easily or quickly. Work carried on after the election to encourage new members, and the NUWSS continued to send deputations to Parliament.

In March, Catherine Osler gave a speech at Queen's College in which she 'pointed out the wonderful advance made by the Society during the last few years', where they had seen membership increase from the start of the century from 120 to over 500 members (60 new members had joined in the previous month alone), and income had already reached £700 for the present year. 24 March saw the publication of the first instalment of Osler's series 'Why Women Need the Vote' in *The Common Cause*. In the articles Osler sets out the suffragists' demands: they did not demand universal suffrage, 'accepting, therefore, without question, the existing basis of the franchise, we merely claim that it should be applied justly and without invidious distinctions – that citizens who fulfil the conditions on which the vote is granted, should not be deprived of it solely on the ground of sex'. In recognition of her long-serving dedication, hard work and sacrifice, Catherine Osler was portrayed on the cover of the 27 October issue of their newspaper: 'Mrs Osler's work for women and girls led her to recognise the paramount importance of securing the enfranchisement of women, and when she found the Liberal Party slack in acting up to its principles she was too good a Liberal to remain within.'

A glimmer of hope appeared in the summer of 1910 when, on 12 July, a Conciliation Bill, designed to give some appeasement to the suffragist movement by giving a limited number of women the vote, was carried through to a second reading in Parliament by 110 votes. If passed, this would extend the vote to women householders, who paid rates and taxes, of which there were around one million. A demonstration intended to keep pressuring the Government was held in London in July, organised jointly by the NUWSS with the WSPU and other suffrage organisations. Three hundred people travelled from the Midlands, including at least 100 from Birmingham: 'They decorated themselves with the colours, and each one carried a flag. They made a very fine show – the nearest approach to a procession there has ever been in Birmingham. The train was covered with placards: "Women's Suffrage – Law-abiding Societies". The engine was a dream of beauty. On each side were two long strings of red, green and white flags, and in front and along the sides were fifteen yards of wreathed evergreen.'[120] Local press coverage acknowledged the role that women played on various boards and committees but still maintained that the right to vote was unnecessary, that many women themselves did not want it and that the potential risk of women voters outnumbering men was unthinkable. *The Birmingham Pictorial & Dart* remarked: 'It must be remembered that the work of such bodies is not legislative, but administrative… Women are not a class… they are adequately represented when their husbands and brothers who are all subject to womanly influence exercise the franchise… Their positions, needs and rights as taxpayers do not differ from that of men and are adequately represented when men vote and men legislate... women outnumber men, this would bring about that the male votes would be swamped... Nor do we think that any but a small minority of the female population want the vote or would trouble to exercise it if they possessed it...'[121]

The pressure on politicians continued throughout the year. In November there were joint deputations of the NUWSS and WSPU to meet local politicians in the Midlands region, which included Sir Francis Lowe, Conservative MP for Edgbaston since 1898. Lowe was reported to have said that he '"did not mind the extension of the franchise to widows and spinsters". This was a concession indeed from any Member for Birmingham'.[122] Perhaps progress was at last being made. Towards the end of the year, however, it became clear that the Government would have to call another election, which would be held from 3 to 19 December, as Asquith's Government aimed to secure a mandate for the Parliament Act of 1911. The Act would prevent the House of Lords from blocking financial legislation, such as the Liberal budget. Learning from their past experiences, and possibly influenced by WSPU tactics and their heavy reliance on propaganda, the BWSS had now identified the best methods of campaigning during this second election. In the report sent to *The Common Cause* for 8 December, it was pointed out that due to there being no marginal seats, 'the committee decided that it was quite useless to work for candidates here, we confined ourselves to propaganda work. We exhibited posters in all parts of the city, and employed sandwichmen throughout the week. We opened two shops for selling the "Common Cause" etc., in which dinner-hour meetings were held... On polling day itself we "manned" twenty-two stations... Six open-air meetings were held... four of these in the Bull Ring drawing large audiences'. The election resulted in the Liberal Party again being short of an overall majority and being forced once more to rely on the Irish nationalists to enable them to form a Government.

The prominence of the BWSS during the two election campaigns of 1910 can be partially explained by the WSPU's decision that January to temporarily cease militant tactics. The result of the first General Election and the Liberal Party's reduced majority meant that the WSPU took 'at face value Asquith's assurance that if a reform bill were to be introduced the Government would make the question of a women's suffrage amendment open to a free vote',[123] and so the WSPU then declared that it would 'use nothing but peaceful and constitutional methods unless the Government adopt an attitude which compels the Union to use more drastic ones. Events may prove that the need of militancy is over'.[124] Locally, the replacement organiser for Gladice Keevil was announced in March as Dorothy Evans, a former gymnastics teacher who had come from Yorkshire, and a new office at 33 Paradise Street was opened. Now recovered from her Winson Green ordeal, Hilda Burkitt had returned to organise meetings at Alum Rock Road and the Bull Ring. The new office was able to remain open until 8pm daily and school room meetings were also being planned to take place in the suburbs: Aston, Handsworth and Small Heath were to be first where work was already in progress, although calls for more canvassers were being issued. This period also saw the adoption of innovative and different ways of campaigning, now necessary to draw attention to the cause while militancy was on hold. The local branch reported on 8 April that 'great amazement and interest has been aroused each day by the band of cycle paraders, carrying posters back and front, to advertise the mission. Twice a day a parade took place, and each time visited a different suburb, where it was always enthusiastically received'. April also saw the inaugural meeting of the Birmingham Men's Political Union for Women's Enfranchisement, a male wing of the WSPU, organised in Birmingham by Harold Wilson of 52 Holly Road, Handsworth.

Although the focus was on winning the right for some women to vote, there was an acknowledgement that women of all classes would benefit from enfranchisement and many campaigners hoped that after it had been awarded to unmarried women householders it would eventually be extended to all women. The plight of women working in factories and in the sweated industries was still a concern for both the WSPU and BWSS. In August 1910 the chain-makers of Cradley Heath, led by Mary Macarthur, founder of the National Federation of Women Workers, had gone on strike in protest against the refusal of employers to award women workers an increased rate of pay as recommend by the Trade Board. As we have seen, the BWSS had already undertaken work amongst this group earlier in the century and now the WSPU took up the workers' cause. In the 2 September issue of *Votes for Women* an article 'The Women Chain-Makers' Strike, The Vote is What We Want', described the terrible conditions of women and children working in this industry, 'the home of one of the worst forms of sweated labour', employing around 1,000 women who worked 12-hour shifts in shops at the back of their homes, for which they typically received 4s or 5s a week, significantly less than the average wage of 9/1d per week reported in 1904 by Cadbury, Matheson and Shann in *Women's Work and Wages*. The strike lasted for 10 weeks.

In December it was reported that the BWSS had begun a class for Social Study, taught by Florence Ring, who had become the BWSS secretary in 1910, and 'has wide experience in social work of various kinds'. Born in Leeds, Florence had married a doctor, William Ring, and had emigrated to Australia in around 1892 where they had two children. William died there in 1894 and Florence and her two children returned to the UK sometime afterwards, as she appears in the 1901 census living in Francis Road, Edgbaston. The first Social Study meeting covered the topic of 'Sweated Home Industries'. *The Common Cause* informed readers that 'the condition of the home workers was described, with special reference to the sweated industries in the Birmingham district. Emphasis was laid on the heavy cost in which sweating involves the nation, both financially and in the moral and physical degeneration of the workers… at the next meeting of the class, the subject of "Sweating Inside the Factories" will be dealt with, and this will be followed by a discussion as to how the vote will be used to combat these conditions'.[125]

Later in the year it was announced by the local WSPU branch that another larger premises had been found for the organisation, near the existing office in Paradise Street, at 97 John Bright Street and supporters were told, 'this is a very excellent central position, being just opposite New Street station and near to so many train termini, and the large window will afford excellent chances of advertisement. The rent, however, is double what it is now, and moving will be a heavy expense'.[126] By November excitement about the Conciliation Bill was building and on 11 November it was announced that the new Birmingham office was ready to open. There were also plans for Mrs Pankhurst to come to the city in November, and 'chalking and special bill distributing will be done on Monday 14 November. A decorative trap will make a circuit of the outskirts of Birmingham'.[127] The following week there was a new, more modern development in the use of propaganda: 'Birmingham has been electrified these few days by the latest method of advertising. The fact that Mrs Pankhurst was speaking in the hall on Tuesday was brought to public notice by means of square lanterns fitted with electric light which shone through, throwing up the words 'Mrs Pankhurst, Town Hall, November 15' in strong relief.'[128] The lanterns were carried through the streets by WSPU volunteers for 11 hours and had been made by members of the Men's Political Union.[129]

On 18 November Asquith announced that the Conciliation Bill was to be dropped, due to the announcement of the second election. This provoked a furious reaction by the suffragettes and a WSPU deputation of 300 women, divided up into detachments of 12 women in each, was sent to Parliament to protest. This episode of suffrage history has come to be known as 'Black Friday', and indeed, the WSPU described its treatment during this event as 'the worst that has been meted out to any deputation since the conflict between women and the Government began'.[130] Birmingham WSPU members present at the demonstration included branch organiser Dorothy Evans, Gladys Hazel, teacher of English and grammar at King Edward's Girls' Grammar School in Aston and now co-organiser alongside Evans, and Isabel Maude Kate Smith, known as Maude Smith, a local woman from Stechford, who, it was reported, 'has worked for her own living since the age of fifteen, and had personal experience of the hardships of women'.[131] Of the Birmingham women at the demonstration, Dorothy Evans was the only one arrested, although no charges were brought against her or any of the others who were detained 'because the Home Office realised that the occasion would be used as a wonderful source of propaganda by the WSPU'.[132]

Maude Smith was interviewed in the 1970s, providing listeners with a vivid picture of her experience in the militant campaign.[133] Maude first learned of the suffragettes through the newspapers and soon after began to purchase *Votes for Women*. She also attended meetings with her friend, Harold Wilson, who helped set up the Men's Political Union in Birmingham, and lived near her in Handsworth. Joining the WSPU under Dorothy Evans' organisation, Maude became a paper-seller, standing in the gutter to sell copies of *Votes for Women*, where she would often have to endure verbal abuse from passers-by. As well as paper-selling, she also helped out in the shop on John Bright Street and was paid £1 a week to do the accounts (she had trained as a bookkeeper before suffering a nervous breakdown that had left her unable to work). Of her experience on deputations to Parliament, Maude remarked that 'the police used to knock us about most cruelly', and she revealed a method that the women had devised of hiding corrugated cardboard under their dresses to prevent the police from getting such a tight grip on them. She also recalled how the police would use men from the East End to assault the women while on demonstration but stated WSPU policy was that 'if there was any suffering, we were to bear it'. The 'Black Friday' protests continued into the following week, where the women began to fight back and threw stones at the windows of Government offices. One of the women who was arrested and charged there was Pattie Hall, who had been involved in the formation of the WSPU in 1903. The Hall family had moved to Birmingham in 1904: Pattie's husband Leonard was a radical journalist and the first vice-chairman of the Independent Labour Party, and they lived at 56 Hagley Road at the time. Her daughter, Nellie, or Emmeline, named after Mrs Pankhurst, had been involved in protests outside Winson Green in September 1909. Pattie was sentenced to 14 days' imprisonment for her part in the 'Black Friday' protests.

The WSPU, like the BWSS, did not actively campaign during the second election in December as there were no marginal seats in Birmingham. Hilda Burkitt was given the task of organising in Dudley, however, which was a target seat, and so she arranged for open-air meetings to be held outside factory gates and in the two markets. Special attention was paid to encouraging working-class voters in Quarry Bank and Cradley Heath to vote against the Liberal candidate. The 9 December issue of *Votes for Women* described that 'Suffragettes were not received well on their first appearance in the town, but after they had been there a week a marvellous change was noticed. Instead of the crowd shouting and booing, they now called for "Three cheers for the Suffragettes and keep the Liberal out"'. On 16 December the results were announced: the Conservative candidate, Major Griffiths-Boscawen, had beaten the Liberal, A. G. Hooper, by 860 votes. The WSPU had supplied 'a decorated wagonette [that] drove about the constituency on polling day to relieve the pickets at the polling stations and the colours were well cheered. Local Liberals seemed to realise that the women had influenced votes, for they were very indignant and, after the poll was declared, tore down the boards from the WSPU Committee Room windows'.[134]

In the local branch reports in *Votes for Women* at this time the same names now begin to recur: Dorothy Evans and Gladys Hazel were the main organisers while Bertha Ryland and Hilda Burkitt were busy helping to run the campaign in and around the city. Bertha in particular was very active at this time, organising throughout the year in Walsall, Leamington Spa, Stafford and Stoke, and meetings and gatherings were often held at the Ryland family home at 19 Hermitage Road, Edgbaston. Gladys Hazel had been an active member of the WSPU since 1909 and had been arrested during a demonstration at Victoria Square in November that year, for protesting at the imprisonment and forcible feeding of Charlotte Marsh after the Bingley Hall incident. After a temporary mistress was employed (at Gladys' own expense) by King Edward's Girls' School while Gladys was on WSPU duties in London, she eventually left her job by mutual agreement in December 1910 and became a full-time organiser alongside Dorothy Evans.

'I am entitled to the vote in the same way as a man'

After the disappointment of the previous months, the campaign received a further blow in the New Year of 1911 when the King's Speech omitted any mention of votes for women. Following the 'Black Friday' incident, militancy had been suspended but the planned census for April that year would afford another opportunity for protest. A boycott was initially proposed by the Women's Freedom League (the organisation formed in 1907 by former WSPU members unhappy with the Pankhurst style of leadership) and the WSPU subsequently decided to participate. Information gathered from the census was required for Lloyd George's National Insurance Bill, in which additional questions were being asked of women that had not appeared in the previous census. This was a major bone of contention for many women, angered by the request for information that would then be used in creating legislation that would directly affect them but in which they would have no say or influence. This included information on how long each married woman in the household had been married for, how many children she had, how many had lived and how many had died. The forms were to be completed by the head of the household, potentially husbands or fathers.

In the 3 March issue of *Votes for Women* the Birmingham office asked for 'the names of those who are willing to take others into their houses on the night of April 2, to allow of a number of women avoiding the census returns… it is intended to hold an all-night party. Particulars of this may be had at the office. All members are cordially invited'. Further information on the Birmingham census evasion was given two weeks later on 24 March and the occasion was now becoming somewhat festive: 'Resisters assemble at the office at 11pm. There will be speeches, a concert, supper, dancing and games, breakfast, chalking parties, baths (Kent Street), and a second breakfast at Lyons' in New Street at 8am.' By the following week open-air meetings had been held all over the district, 'everywhere the words 'No Vote No Census' have been chalked, and people are being told about the census protest'.[135] *The Birmingham Pictorial & Dart* included at the end of March an illustration titled 'Spoiling His Census Paper', the caption read 'A number of Suffragettes in Birmingham, it is said, will avoid filling in the schedules for their houses. "No Vote.-No Census", will be written across them'.[136]

Many of the names of WSPU members active in Birmingham do not appear in the census returns. This includes Hilda Burkitt, Bertha Ryland and Maude Smith, all of whom were presumably at the evasion party, the address of which is still unknown.[137] The census return for the Hall family, living on Hagley Road, also cannot be found. Gladys Hazel wrote on her schedule 'Votes for Women', 'No Votes No Census', and the enumerator noted on the return that the housekeeper informed him that Miss Hazel did not sleep at the property on Harold Road, Edgbaston, on the night the census was taken. In addition to those noted by Jill Liddington and Elizabeth Crawford in *Vanishing for the Vote*, there are another two notable returns from Birmingham: Alice M. Clarke, who lived at 90 Nursery Road, Lozells, with her husband and three young children, completed the census but gave her occupation as 'suffragette'; likewise 20-year-old student Constance Estcourt and her younger sister Doris Estcourt, a school pupil, living with their family at 38 George Road, Edgbaston, both gave their occupation as 'suffragette'.

A week after the census was taken *Votes for Women* included an account of the evasion that Rhoda Anstey, Head of Anstey Physical Training College in Erdington, had undertaken on behalf of herself and her students. Titled 'Head of a College Resists', Anstey explained that she was a suffragist and had previously avoided participating in the militant movement. However, 'this Census protest… is a thing I am able to do without injury to anyone except myself. It is extremely unpleasant to me to commit an unlawful act in this way, but while others have made such tremendous sacrifices I must not shrink from this small one, especially as I am told that an open protest such as I propose to make will be a real help to the cause'. She explained further: 'My position is this: I am a ratepayer, and in my opinion – and in the opinion of the majority of thinking people in this country – I am entitled to the Vote in the same way as a man. The Vote has been asked for and continually refused. I therefore refuse to answer this demand of the Government, not in any spirit of retaliation, but as a protest – the only protest I, a vote-less ratepayer, can use to let them know what I feel and think… One reason why women are making this protest is that this Census will furnish statistics on which will be based further legislation for women workers; this legislation women do *not* want until they themselves have a voice in the matter.'[138] Anstey had refused to answer the questions on the census return and wrote on the form 'No Vote No Census! I protest against the injustice done to women rate-payers by the continued refusal of the Government to give them the vote, and hereby refuse to fill in the census forms for my household.' Rhoda Anstey, Principal of Anstey College. Note 'If the Conciliation Bill passes the 3rd Reading on 5 May I undertake to give the information desired'.[139]

While the NUWSS did not agree with the boycott (Catherine Osler, head of her household after the death of her husband, Alfred, returned a completed schedule), the return for Florence Ring, BWSS secretary and close friend of Catherine Osler, is intriguing. While Florence did complete her schedule she made sure that her profession as secretary for the Women's Suffrage Society was recorded and not only supplied her home address of 169 Bristol Road, but also her work address, the BWSS office at 10 Easy Row. While the protest did attract publicity it is difficult to judge how effective it was as a tactic within the wider campaign and the Liberal Government decided not to prosecute any of the evaders, arguing that the enumerators had gathered sufficient data and the number of actual evaders was 'negligible'.[140]

Although militancy was not being used at this time by the WSPU, the advantages gained by being prepared to use it were discussed in an article by Christabel Pankhurst, published in *Votes for Women* on 14 April. In 'The Ethics of Militancy', Christabel argued that the power of the WSPU to use militancy gave their campaign strength in the face of defeat (the next Conciliation Bill was due to be discussed in May that year): 'it is with us always the case that the moment of apparent defeat is the moment where our pride is highest and our determination most strong'. The Bill was debated in May and won a majority of 255 to 88 as a Private Members' Bill and was promised a week of Government time. However, November 1911 saw Asquith now announce the Manhood Suffrage Bill, which would increase the male franchise but would not extend it to women (the Bill was subsequently dropped). In response the WSPU organised another deputation to Westminster to take place on 21 November. Militancy was now resumed in earnest and the demonstration escalated to window-smashing at multiple Government buildings on Whitehall and Parliament Street, including the Home Office, the War Office and the Treasury. The incident resulted in 220 women and three men being arrested, including Bertha Ryland, who was tried three days later and sentenced to seven days' imprisonment in Holloway Prison. On the return to militancy Catherine Osler commented in the BWSS annual report, 'unhappily the militant suffragists by their deplorable window breaking tactics played into the hands of our enemies and gave weak-kneed and half-hearted supporters an excuse to break their pledges, of which they were not slow to avail themselves'.[141]

'Our only weapon is militancy'

In the first edition of *Votes for Women* for the New Year the position of the WSPU was made clear: 'our only weapon in 1912, as in former years, until our demand is conceded, is militancy'.[142] Early 1912 saw the introduction of the Parliamentary Franchise (Women) Bill with a second reading planned for the end of March. Another window-smashing campaign had already begun on the evening of 1 March, undertaken purely with the intention of attracting press attention and keeping pressure on the Government to pass the Bill. Women armed with stones, sticks and hammers went on the rampage over the next few days, targeting West End shops and Government buildings, including 10 Downing Street. A pamphlet by Christabel Pankhurst called 'Broken Windows', published that year, declared that 'the message of the broken pane is that women are determined that the lives of their sisters shall no longer be broken, and that in the future those who have to obey the law shall have a voice in saying what that law shall be. Repression cannot break the spirit of liberty'.[143] On 8 March some familiar names were committed for trial: Bertha Ryland and Maude Smith had been arrested, along with Gladys Hazel, Dorothy Evans and Hilda Burkitt, for smashing the windows of commercial properties in and around Old Bond Street. All were given substantial sentences of between four and six months. Gladys Hazel's papers give an intimate sense of what the experience was like for these mainly middle-class women, embroiled in acts of militancy, recalling that she 'had never enjoyed anything so much in my life'.[144] On 29 March it was stated that during her trial Bertha Ryland, who had been convicted for the same offence the previous November, 'enquired whether she would be treated under the new prison rules. The judge replied that he did not know; he had merely to pass the sentence of imprisonment. She would not be in the second division, but would be treated not quite in the same way as hard labour prisoners'.[145] At the end of the month, the Conciliation Bill was narrowly defeated by 14 votes. The WSPU rejected claims that it was their militancy that had caused the defeat and blamed the eight members of the Government who, had they voted for the Bill, would have carried it through: their eight votes would have counted as 16 under existing Parliamentary rules.[146]

The length of sentence that Bertha received as well as the decision not to classify the imprisoned women as political prisoners was cause for great concern, not least by members of her own family. In a letter dated 8 April 1912 sent by Bertha's brother, Henry, to Francis Newdegate, MP for Tamworth, he wrote: 'We do not allege that my sister did not smash a window but what we complain about is the undue severity of the sentence, six months.' The damage was estimated at a cost of £6. Henry compared Bertha's crime to a similar incident which occurred in Birmingham when an unemployed man had smashed a window of Lloyds Bank on Colmore Row, valued at £100, and had only received one month's imprisonment: 'Is this British justice?' Henry asked. He also protested that Bertha should be classed as a political prisoner, warning that 'if these concessions are not granted in all probability the hunger strikes, which previously won them, will be resumed'.[147]

The 10 May issue of *Votes for Women* included an article titled 'Torture in English Prisons'. Bertha and Maude served much of their sentences at Winson Green so it is possible that the article refers to one of them: 'From the Birmingham prison also comes grave news of a Suffragist prisoner who has been brutally and shamefully treated. She was forcibly fed for three weeks, and fed while in irons for over twenty-four hours. They bruised her all over till she was black and blue; six heavy wardresses set on her and handcuffed her hands behind her back. She was kept hidden away in hospital so that the other Suffragists in prison should know nothing of what was going on.' Local press coverage offered an alternative view. In an article titled 'A Judicial Farce', the *Birmingham Daily Mail* gave the following guileless description of the treatment the women were said to be receiving in Winson Green Gaol: 'It is understood they are simply amusing themselves, or passing away the time by sewing, crocheting, or knitting.'[148] In her 1975 interview, Maude Smith talks eloquently about her prison experience, painting a very different picture from the one given by the *Birmingham Daily Mail*.[149] She was only able to keep a diary by smuggling in a pencil in the hem of her skirt and writing on toilet paper (sadly the diary no longer existed when she was interviewed), but she was given some books and was allowed to sew. There was no heating in the cells, however, and they were expected to sleep on wooden planks. Any exercise that they were permitted to do ceased once the women went on hunger strike. While prison conditions were horrendous enough to endure, it is Maude's description of being forcibly fed that is most harrowing. She recalled that the feeding tube was forced up her nostrils, 'if it will go', in her words, which caused her permanent damage, and she still suffered from nosebleeds 60 years later. She also suffered from colitis. Food would be poured down her throat that had not been properly cooked or softened enough so this naturally caused her excruciating pain, a 'feeling like being thrown across the room'. Maude resisted for as long as she could but towards the end she became unable to fight. This treatment was carried out three times a day.

A collection of documents in the National Archives reveals much about Hilda Burkitt's experience, also sentenced to four months' imprisonment, to be served in Holloway Prison.[150] In a petition made to the Liberal Government on 15 June, Hilda requested that: 'Whereas the leaders of the Women's Social & Political Union, Mrs Pankhurst and Mr and Mrs Pethick Lawrence have now received their rights as Political Offenders, and have been placed in the First Division, I hereby claim that all the women who are at present suffering imprisonment for this same cause including myself should receive the same treatment and be at once placed in the 1st Division as we are all in prison for the same object, namely, to obtain the Enfranchisement of Women.' At the end of June a phone call was made from the prison to the Home Office to report that Hilda had been in hospital under observation for the past six weeks: 'she is mentally very unstable, but physically she is all right'. She had been refusing food and the doctor recommended that 'owing to her doubtless hysterical condition' she should not be forcibly fed but released immediately.

There were further outbreaks of militancy as the year progressed but these were not without impact on the wider organisation. On 5 July it was declared: 'Militancy has broken out again! … In Parliament last Friday a truce to militancy was suggested. The WSPU has called a truce on more than one occasion in the past, but the Government have exploited and abused this forbearance. Even if the Union were to call a truce, militancy would still go on, because there are women who have made up their minds never again to put faith in faithless politicians, and never again to cease from strife until the Vote is actually won.'[151] However, militant tactics were not felt by all involved with the WSPU to be an effective campaigning tool and fractures began to appear within the organisation. Emmeline and Frederick Pethick Lawrence were the first victims of this: both were expelled from the organisation by Christabel for disagreeing with the extreme methods now being employed. Christabel had escaped arrest after 'Black Friday' by fleeing to Paris, where she would remain until 1914. Bertha Ryland was released from prison in early July. The campaign continued throughout the year and in November it was reported that 'various pillar-boxes in the Birmingham areas… have been damaged by Suffragettes. The time-plates were smashed, and inside the boxes were found slips marked "Votes for Women"'.[152] Later on telephone wires began to be attacked. Referring to letterbox arson, the new suffrage newspaper edited by Christabel in Paris, *The Suffragette*, gave this explanation: 'They want to make the elector and the Government so uncomfortable that, in order to put an end to the nuisance, they will give women the vote… The vote has never been given as a prize for good conduct. Women will never get the vote except by creating an intolerable situation for the selfish and pathetic people who stand in their way.'[153] This was a sign of things to come. From 1913 the targets of the militants would become more outrageous, the tactics they used would become more risky, and the consequences they faced would become more serious.

The peak of militancy: 1913-1914

'We are militant because only so can the Vote be won'

Bertha Ryland, 1914

A peaceful pilgrimage

Against a backdrop of escalating militancy, the Birmingham Women's Suffrage Society continued campaigning using constitutional means. A Reform Bill came before Parliament in January 1913 but although 'the previous months had been ones of intense activity for the NUWSS's chief organisers: a series of women's amendments had been drafted, each providing for a varying degree of enfranchisement for women',[154] these amendments were later withdrawn after the Speaker of the House ruled that any alterations to the Bill that included women's suffrage would mean it would have to be presented as a new Bill and sent back for a second reading, leading to disappointment once more. After similar setbacks in 1910 and 1911, the NUWSS had begun to reconsider its political position. The Labour Party was now becoming more committed to women's suffrage and this led, in May 1912, to the NUWSS establishing an Election Fighting Fund, a special fund which would be used to raise money for the support of Labour candidates in any three-cornered elections and to enable building a Labour Party election machine in selected constituencies in which the NUWSS hoped to persuade Labour to fight, particularly those held by leading Liberals if they were anti-suffragist.[155] In Birmingham, 'Catherine Osler supported the national executive in this, although by no means all local societies did. Birmingham was still radical'.[156]

Despite the failure to include women's suffrage in the Reform Bill, the BWSS's annual report for 1912-13 suggested that there was still a sense of optimism that the vote might come soon and that women should prepare themselves for this through education and social justice work: the BWSS asserted that 'the outlook for the immediate future is one which calls for steadiness of purpose, loyalty and courage in the face of temporary check and delay'. As a long-standing suffrage organisation, they recognised their duty 'to create a strong public opinion in favour of justice to women, and at the same time to deepen the sense of national responsibility in the minds of women themselves, that they may take pains to qualify themselves for a wide exercise of the vote when they get it by acquiring a sound knowledge of public matters, especially those affecting the lives of their own sex and of children, and by training themselves in social and political work'.[157]

The NUWSS's most ambitious project of 1913 was a national Pilgrimage held during the summer. It would cross the country and culminate in a huge gathering in London, taking advantage of their enormous membership. By this time the NUWSS could boast around 50,000 members; in comparison the WSPU only ever had around 2,000 members.[158] The main aim of the Pilgrimage was to reinforce the distinction between the constitutional campaign and the militant one but, by doing this through the creation of a large, headline-attracting spectacle, the NUWSS was clearly taking inspiration from the more publicity-aware WSPU. The Pilgrimage took six weeks in total, beginning on 18 June at Land's End, and finishing at Hyde Park in London on 26 July. At the final gathering there were approximately 50,000 people present and 19 platforms were set up to enable attendees to hear the speakers, which included Millicent Fawcett. The Pilgrimage passed through the Midlands in July. On the 14th the *Birmingham Daily Mail* carried a report of the arrival of the pilgrims in Birmingham: 'At 5 o'clock a strong contingent of the Birmingham Women's Suffrage Society marched from Easy Row to meet the pilgrims who had started early in the afternoon from Wolverhampton. At Great King Street, Hockley, the visitors were joined by the local suffragists, and a procession was formed, headed by the Baskerville Band. Banners bearing the legends 'Law-Abiding' and 'By Reason, Not Force' were prominently displayed.'

The Pilgrimage was well received by the press and was recognised as a spectacle worthy of coverage. The *Staffordshire Advertiser* commented: 'The successful carrying out of an effort on so large a scale has demonstrated among other things the organising power within the National Union. From first to last some thousands of members of the National Union have taken part in the effort, hundreds of meetings and many tens of thousands of people have been addressed, over half a million leaflets have been distributed, and over £7,800 has been collected or subscribed.' Continuing the work that they had undertaken a few years earlier with textile and chain workers, one of the speakers declared that the Pilgrimage was not just for their own benefit but that 'they were fighting for women who from their very need were debarred from fighting for themselves, the women in the slums and in the factories, and they fought with constitutional weapons, because they believed that a cause founded on right and justice should only be advanced by righteous methods'.[159]

The feeling that real progress was now being made was supported by Asquith's meeting in August with a deputation led by Fawcett. The Prime Minister remarked: 'I quite recognise that the request which you put forward, after the recent law-abiding demonstration of your societies, has a special claim on my consideration and stands upon

Both forcible feeding, and the so-called Cat and Mouse Act of 1913 (which permitted hunger-striking women to be released from prison on licence until they recovered and were re-imprisoned) were emotive political issues in the pre-war years.

Medals were presented to suffragettes who had undertaken hunger strikes in prison, commemorating their endurance and dedication to the cause.

THE SUFFRAGETTES GET WILDER DAILY
& SMASH SHOP WINDOWS. OH! SO GAILY

Window-smashing was an early militant tactic by the suffragettes, who targeted both political and commercial institutions, and often received disproportionately harsh sentences for their actions.

F.A. New degate Esq. M.P

19, HERMITAGE ROAD,
EDGBASTON.
april 8th . 12

Dear Sir
my mother being seriously unwell has asked me to reply to your letter.
We do not allege that my sister did not smash a window but what we complain about is the undue severity of the sentence, six months.
The damage done was reported in the official organ of the W.S.P.U "Votes for Women" to be £ 6.0.0.
To show the cruel severity of this sentence I should like to point out that a working man, being out of work, as a protest, presumably, smashed two large panes of glass at Lloyds Bank Colmore Row Birmingham valued at over £ 100.0.0 he was sentenced to one month's imprisonment. Is this British justice?

Bertha's brother, Henry Ryland, protests to a local MP, Francis Newdegate, at Bertha's long sentence for window-smashing in 1912.

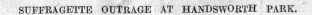

SUFFRAGETTE OUTRAGE AT HANDSWORTH PARK.

THE BURNED BOATS AND THE REMAIN[...]

SUFFRAGETTE OUTRAGE AT KING'S NORTON.

1913-1914 saw a number of serious arson attacks by suffragette groups in the West Midlands, including Handsworth Boathouse, Northfield Library and train carriages at King's Norton Station.

NORTHFIELD SUFFRAGETTE OUTRAGE.

THE RUINS OF THE CARNEGIE LIBRARY AT NORTHFIELD, BURNED BY SUFFRAGETTES.

[Photo: "Birmingham Daily Mail."]

THE MYSTERIOUS FIFTY!

BIRMINGHAM BAND TO RETALIATE ON SUFFRAGETTES.

If all that we are told be true, there is in existence in Birmingham a powerful little organisation for dealing with Suffragettes—one which does not believe in half-measures by any means. Its aims and objects are revealed in an amusing letter to the editor of the "Gazette."

The writer refers to our report of the act of retaliation at the Suffragette offices in John Bright-street. The "mud," he says (we presume our correspondent is a male), was black paint mixed with acid,

and the notice, in addition to the words "We remember the park outrage," also bore the Latin inscription: "Lex talionis. Fas est et ab hoste docere."—The law of revenge. It is right to derive instruction even from an enemy."

We heartily apologise for our omission, but the fact is that the painter, whoever he was, had "laid it on so thick," to use a colloquialism, that the Latin referred to, although on the back of the paper, was absolutely indecipherable.

Below is a reproduction of the letter:

Monday morning.
"Suffragettes"
Dear Editor.

Your report re "Tit for tat" was to a certain extent correct except for the fact that the "mud" was Black paint mixed with acid, and you omitted to publish the Latin which was also written on the back of the paper.

We shall always use the same paper for our work as this upon which we have given you a "sample."

We have a first rate "programme" for the summer and we will give you "copy" from time to time.

We intended totally destroying the premises last night, (but the policeman happened to be too near,) but you can take it for granted that we shall make them sorry for what they have done to "Birmingham"

We have succeeded in making bombs which will be far in advance of any they have had so far and as they have a shroud maker over their premises they will be able to leave their orders "as they go up."

We have any amount of money at our disposal and together with our "knowledge', should manage to give the public some good interesting reading from day to day.

We shall not be responsible for the safety of any person whom we know (and we have many in sight) to be con-

nected with these outrages, and the cost of the damage to our Cathedral will be revenged twenty-fold

Part of the Programme— will be as follows.

Total destruction of their Headquarters

Personal disfigurement either by acid or cutting off of their hair, (easy by kidnapping)

Bomb for Bomb

Destruction of clothes by acid

Binding and gagging after being rendered unconscious by fumes (better than prison)

Destruction of premises found harbouring them or their literature.

Tarring and feathering

Branding of the face. etc;
(other list at our next meeting)

If the police cannot put this insensible method of advertisement down, we shall not only help them, but also take the matter in our own hands. There will be no danger to the public nor to any animals by the methods we have in view.

We are over fifty strong and have a motor or two. and at our meeting on Saturday night decided to make a start, being of the opinion that once we start, others will follow.

The public are crying for

"REVENGE"

THEY SHALL HAVE IT

We're
Satisfied   Number One (of the "Fifty")
Prisons
Useless

The 'Mysterious Fifty' publish their alarming manifesto for retaliation against the suffragettes. *Birmingham Daily Gazette,* March 1914.

NO. 21,844 (Founded 1741)   £1,000

BY FIRE AND PAINT!

THREE OUTRAGES IN BIRMINGHAM.

RAILWAY COACHES FIRED.

EIGHT DESTROYED

CATHEDRAL DAUBED WITH PAINT.

PAVILION GUTTED.

Three serious outrages by militant Suffragettes are reported in Birmingham to-day.

Eight passenger coaches on a Midland Railway siding at King's Norton were destroyed by fire last night.

A disgraceful outrage to the Cathedral Church was discovered early yesterday. It is supposed that someone was secreted in the building on Saturday after evensong and later opened the vestry door and admitted other persons.

The phrases, "Votes for Women," "Stop forcibly feeding," and similar expressions, were daubed in white paint over practically every spot within reach from floor to ceiling.

The Olton lawn tennis pavilion was destroyed by fire on Friday night. damage to the extent of £300 was caused. A copy of a Suffragist newspaper was found near the building.

KING'S NORTON FIRE.

with the words "Stop forcible feeding."

After the services yesterday knots of people gathered outside the Cathedral and discussed the latest outrage, the almost unanimous feeling being one of profound disgust towards the perpetrators of it. One prominent Churchman was heard to say that this latest act of militancy had, he should imagine, finally alienated any sympathy which Churchgoers in Birmingham might have held towards the militant Suffragettes.

Verger's Story.

One of the Cathedral vergers in an interview with a "Gazette" representative last night, said that there was only a congregation of about twenty at evensong on Saturday night, and these for the most part were women. There was plenty of opportunity for the militants to have secreted themselves in the gallery after the service until the vergers had left the church and locked all the doors. Therefore the intruders were left with the whole of the night in order to complete their work of desecration. This completed, they had left the church by means of one of the vestry doors which could be opened from the inside but not from without.

In reply to questions by our representative, the verger declared that he noticed nothing in the least suspicious about the women who attended the service on Saturday evening, and so far as he knew none of them carried bags in which the paint and brushes could be hidden.

Workmen will to-day be engaged in removing all traces of paint from the building. In cases where desecration on a much smaller scale has been committed, churches have been re-consecrated, but it is not yet known whether such a course will be taken with the Cathedral.

OUTRAGE AT OLTON.

TENNIS PAVILION DESTROYED BY FIRE.

Another outrage was committed by Suffragettes in Birmingham on Friday night, when the Olton Lawn Tennis Club's pavilion was destroyed by fire.

At 10.30, when the outbreak was first discovered, the flames had secured a good hold on the building, and when the Solihull Fire Brigade, who had been summoned, appeared on the scene they could do very little. A copy of a Suffragette newspaper was found affixed to some wire near the pavilion. The damage is put at about £300.

TIT FOR TAT!

RETALIATION AT SUFFRAGETTE HEADQUARTERS.

Late last night the window and the door of the Suffragist offices in John Bright-street, Birmingham were discovered by a policeman to be well plastered in mud, and with a notice pasted on the door bearing the following announcement:—

We remember the Park outrage. More will follow.

The *Birmingham Daily Gazette* rounds up a series of suffragette 'outrages' committed in the West Midlands in March 1914. suffragette militancy was at its peak.

John Bensley Thornhill as a Boy,
George Romney *c*.1784-5.

113

state that the attendants have exercised the keenest supe
vision during the last six weeks, but an outrage of this
character is quite unpreventable

A photograph showing the damage done is submitted
herewith:-

The Keeper added that he was in London at the time of the
outrage, but that the Assistant Keeper, on the authority of Mr
W.A.Cadbury, had the Gallery closed immediately.

269.   RESOLVED: That the action of the Assistant Keeper
in closing the Gallery be approved, and that the Gallery be kept
closed until after the ordinary meeting of the Committee on
Monday next.

The Keeper submitted certain suggestions for additional
protection of the Galleries and further suggestions were made
by members of the Committee.

Photograph © Museum of Fine Arts Boston. George Romney,
1734 - 1802, *John Thornhill (1773 - 1841) as a Boy*, Museum of
Fine Arts, Boston. Given in memory of Governor Alvan T. Fuller
by the Fuller Foundation 61.962

The damage inflicted on the painting by
Bertha Ryland is no longer visible in the
restored painting, but can clearly be seen
on a contemporary photograph in the
museum minute book from 1914.

72

Maude Smith, long-term WSPU Birmingham member, on trial for attacking a painting at the National Gallery, 1914. She was tried under the pseudoym Mary Spencer, a commonly adopted tactic to evade the harsh sentences handed out to repeat suffragette offenders.

Right to serve demonstration in London.

Women joined men working in Birmingham's munitions factories during the war effort, 1915-1918.

Mary Macarthur and Margery Corbett Ashby. Seasoned political campaigners, they stood in West Midlands constituencies in the first Parliamentary election to permit female candidates in 1918, although neither won.

Christabel Pankhurst campaigning in Smethwick during the 1918 election. Despite considerable political backing, she failed to win the seat.

another footing from similar demands proceeding from other quarters, where a different method and spirit prevails.' His tone was clearly conciliatory, and represented the first indication of a possible shift in attitude on his part.[160] This 'different method and spirit' referred to the reception Asquith had received the previous month on a visit to Birmingham, where he had again felt the full force of WSPU militancy. The 1913-14 BWSS report reflected on the Pilgrimage, proclaiming success in its objective of distinguishing in the minds of the general public between their organisation and the WSPU: 'No longer is the original and constitutional Suffrage movement confused with the more recent and militant section; and if nothing but a clearer understanding on this point has resulted, the Pilgrimage would have justified itself. But it did much more. Its effect on the minds of Politicians was undeniably great. After the vast gathering in Hyde Park, which marked its culmination on 26 July, Mr Asquith consented to receive a deputation and his attitude on that occasion is said to have exhibited a marked change.'[161]

The following year it was reported that there were now 774 members of the BWSS, with 155 new members signing up that year. In all, 131 meetings had been held, including 52 working people's meetings and 21 meetings with Men's Trade Unions, continuing and building on the links that had been made earlier with the chain and nail makers of Cradley Heath and showing support for the Labour Party through the Election Fighting Fund. These meetings were often challenging for BWSS organisers though, as 'they mainly consisted of men, were held in public houses and often late at night. However, the BWSS were convinced that the working classes appreciated their constitutional methods and that their work was being rewarded when the unions began to give visible support to the suffrage both on a local and national level'.[162] The Society also set up a mechanism for those who could not afford to subscribe but wanted to be involved with the campaign, thereby supporting and engaging with working-class women. The 'Friends of Women's Suffrage' had, by 1913, 1,600 members across the country, 'mainly working-class women who could not afford to pay the annual membership fee but were prepared to sign pledges of support'.[163] While the policy of the NUWSS had changed so that they now worked to support Labour candidates and were strengthening bonds with the unions, they stuck with the policy of votes for women on equal terms as men, although there were radical suffragists within the organisation who wanted equal voting rights for all women. Indeed, many former members of the NUWSS had become involved with organisations like the Women's Co-operative Guild and trade unions, calling for 'womanhood suffrage' – a vote for every adult woman regardless of property qualification.

Cat and mouse

In early 1913 *The Suffragette* newspaper included an article by Edith Kerwood, who had been involved with the Birmingham WSPU since 1907 (and was one of the first members from the city to be arrested during the deputation to Parliament of that year). In 'How I Became a Militant', Kerwood observed: 'In spite of all the joy and beauty of civilised life, yet it seems to me that the world is out of joint, and I am convinced that it will never be put right till women are free to express themselves and bring about a better and nobler social order... I am unshaken in my firm belief that the militancy of women is right. They are showing far more moderation and restraint than men would do under similar circumstances, and behind the violence and the aggressive acts that are in themselves so distasteful, I see the moral strength and courage and the spiritual insight that nothing can crush.'[164] The need for militancy to be justified became even more pressing at this time. That violent women were viewed differently from men carrying out similar actions is clear: the sight of middle-class, leisured women suddenly taking up arms in the form of hammers and stones would have been shocking for many and their lawlessness was roundly condemned by politicians and newspapers, while others saw the employment of such tactics as damaging to the cause. However, the most typical response, particularly in the press, was to belittle the women and accuse them of being childish or not of sound mind, and therefore not to be trusted with something as serious as the vote. In an article in *The Times* from the previous year, referring to the window-smashing campaign, the writer remarked: 'Whatever may be the thought of the suffragist agitation its immediate grievance is simply infantile.'[165] Contemporary postcards from the time further demonstrate that the suffrage cause was a source of amusement and contempt, for example, 'Beauty and Intellect are Superior to Brute Force' and 'The Wild Rose, which requires careful handling'.

However, the WSPU now had another problem to deal with. In the spring of 1913 the Prisoners (Temporary Discharge for Ill-Health) Bill was introduced, specifically to address the ongoing issue of hunger-striking suffragettes and the public outcry over forcible feeding. Women who had been on hunger strike in prison would now be released on licence just before they became seriously ill and then re-arrested once they had partially recovered. *Votes for Women* described it in their 14 March issue as 'The Cat and Mouse Bill', which was 'designed to deal in a new manner with Suffrage prisoners by releasing them after the hunger strike and re-arresting them, when they are sufficiently recovered, to serve a second term'. The writer continued: 'We can well believe that the Cabinet are disinclined to give more publicity than they can help to this discreditable device, which more closely resembles the methods of a cat torturing a mouse than the attempts of statesmen to deal with their political opponents.'

In the build-up to introducing the 'Cat and Mouse Act', late 1912 had seen an increase in the number of arson attacks in Birmingham and in other cities across the country as the Government's position became more entrenched and the militant campaign intensified in response. Birmingham was not particularly unique in the trend for militant activities but some of the targets and types of incidents stand out as unusual. While many acts of militancy were carried out by women acting on their own, the planning and execution of such daring and often dangerous acts may have occurred due to the strong relationships that would have existed between the women involved in the campaign at the time, many of them having worked alongside one another for a number of years, enabling the building of trust between members necessary for carrying out such actions. The local branch would also have been revitalised by the arrival in the summer of 1913 of Lilias Mitchell, the new area organiser. Lilias came from a prosperous Edinburgh family and had been working for the cause for a number of years. In 1907 she had gone with her mother to hear Emmeline Pankhurst speak at a meeting. Both mother and daughter were overwhelmed with enthusiasm for the cause: 'We felt completely lifted out of ourselves, joined the Society there and then and went home walking it seemed on air.'[166] One of the more infamous incidents Lilias was involved with was the removal of marker flags at the golf course at Balmoral, the royal residence in the Highlands of Scotland, which were then replaced with flags in the WSPU colours.

On 31 January there were five pillar box arsons in Birmingham and, on the next day, five cases of golf course vandalism: although Lilias Mitchell had not yet arrived in the Midlands in person, the action undertaken by her at Balmoral influenced similar incidents across the country and, indeed, sites of male-dominated sporting and leisure activities were frequently targeted by the WSPU. Pillar box arson proved particularly popular and continued throughout the year. There were also disturbances during services at St Philip's and St Martin's churches and telephone wires were cut in public call boxes. In April, an attempt to burn down Handsworth boathouse was made but the fire was extinguished before any serious damage was caused. One of the more unusual incidents in the Midlands occurred in this year, when there was an attempted explosion of the canal bank near Yardley Wood. While arson and the planting of bombs were tactics that were being used up and down the country, this is possibly the only attack on a canal bank that the suffragettes attempted. *The Staffordshire Advertiser* reported on 28 June 1913: 'The Birmingham police have received information of what is believed to be an attempt on the part of suffragists to blow up the embankment of the Birmingham and Stratford-on-Avon Canal. Mr Sale, who lives in Lime Kiln-lane, Pool Hill, noticed a heap of debris in the lane which runs along the bottom of the canal embankment, and on examination he found a deep gap in the crown. It was about 5ft. across, 8ft. or 9ft. long, and extended down to about 3in. from the water line. Near the gap was found a spud shovel and a length of fuse, and later some children picked up a sheet of paper on which was written "Votes for women; mind your canals". Mr Sale states there was every indication that an explosion had taken place, a hole had apparently been bored in the embankment from the waterside, the explosive had been fixed, and the fuse attached. Had the hole been dug into the embankment from the other side below the water line, it is believed a breach would have been made which would have liberated the water for a stretch of 11 miles. There is no lock. A day or two before the discovery two women and a man were seen examining the embankment, but no notice was taken of them.'

The interview with Birmingham WSPU member Maude Smith, recorded in 1975, sheds some light on this incident.[167] Maude recalled that at some point during her time as a WSPU member she was sent to collect explosives from a house in Coventry, which she then brought back on the train to be stored in the basement at John Bright Street. She confirmed that the WSPU had its own recipes for making explosives, although they were not very strong. Maude then described going with a young man (this could possibly have been her friend and member of the Men's Political Union, Harold Evans) to the canal to set the explosives, after they had had an earlier trial run in a garden somewhere which reportedly blew a hole in the lawn. At the canal a hole was dug in the bank, into which they planted the bomb, and they then returned home. Maude confirmed in the interview that the bomb did explode but that it only blew a hole in the bank and did not pierce the basin. As the news report stated, had the bank exploded the consequences could have been catastrophic, potentially resulting in the loss of life, something that the WSPU had previously always been careful to avoid. The incident suggests that WSPU members were becoming increasingly desperate at this point, adopting more and more risky behaviour in order to continue attracting the attention of both press and politicians.

In July 1913 Prime Minister Asquith had made another trip to Birmingham, a couple of weeks after the NUWSS Pilgrimage had passed through the city, but was met with a similar reaction to the one he received in 1909 at Bingley Hall. Over the course of two days there were seven pillar box arson attacks, two cases of house arson, and window-smashing of properties on Colmore Row and at the Grand Hotel where Mr Asquith was dining. Eight women were arrested in connection with the incidents. In addition, 'false fire alarms were given, and Mr Asquith was questioned on his attitude to Women Suffrage by men sympathisers with the movement'.[168] One of the women arrested was Nellie Hall, daughter of Pattie Hall, the friend of Emmeline Pankhurst who had been arrested in 1912 for window-smashing. Nellie was charged with throwing a brick though the window of Asquith's car and was sentenced to three weeks in prison but released eight days later on licence under the 'Cat and Mouse Act' after commencing a hunger strike.[169]

Militancy continued throughout the year. In October, a Sunday service at St Philip's was interrupted by a number of suffragettes who were seated in a side gallery. At the end of the service they all 'chanted in unison… the following prayer:- "God save Sylvia Pankhurst, Mary Richardson,[170] and all Suffragist prisoners, save them, save them! Their enemies torture them, they are all persecuted, they suffer for conscience sake. Spare them, spare them; hear us when we pray to Thee!" Every eye was turned towards them, but no attempt was made to eject them, and when they had finished their prayer they walked quietly out of the building'.[171] This was one of a series of demonstrations that now targeted churches. At the end of October *The Suffragette* included a one-page article titled 'The Deplorable Apathy of the Church' and gave details of a number of recent interruptions to church services across the country.[172]

That same month Emmeline Pankhurst gave a speech titled 'Why We Are Militant' during a trip to New York, herself on licence from prison at the time under the 'Cat and Mouse Act'. Reminding her listeners of the violence used by men during the Chartist movement of the 1830s and 1840s, Pankhurst justified the use of such action by the WSPU: 'Men got the vote because they were and would be violent. The women did not get it because they were constitutional and law-abiding… we have been so accustomed, we women, to accept one standard for men and another standard for women, that we have even applied that variation of standard to the injury of our political welfare.' They were being forced into using aggressive tactics: 'The only justification for risk to the comfort of other human beings is the fact that you have tried all other available means and have failed to secure justice.'[173] There was clearly a sense of unease felt by the authorities about women who were prepared to go to such extremes of behaviour. Unfortunately, violence was met with violence, as the Government persisted in forcibly feeding suffragette prisoners.

'The fire and sword of active rebellion'
The campaign in Birmingham, again reflective of the wider campaign, continued to escalate. Under the leadership of Lilias Mitchell, militant action in the city intensified, becoming even more audacious. There were 27 separate incidents in the city and surrounding areas leading up to August 1914. Most notably, this included the burning down of the Carnegie Library (now Northfield Library) on 11 February, which destroyed around 1,500 books:

the damage was estimated at nearly £2,000, according to *The Suffragette* in an article titled 'The Sword of Damocles'. The library had opened in 1906 after Andrew Carnegie had donated £5,000 towards the opening of ten free libraries in the city and the land was donated to the corporation by George Cadbury. This attack coincided with the opening of Parliament. The culprits left a copy of *The Suffragette* with the message 'Give Women the Vote' written on it along with Christabel Pankhurst's pamphlet 'The Great Scourge and How to End It' and a note saying 'To start your new library'. The burning down of Northfield Library appears to be the only example of library arson by suffragettes nationally, although there had been an earlier attempt to burn down Tipton Library in the Black Country a few months before. On that occasion, the librarian had discovered a piece of candle and a quantity of wax concealed in the woodwork of the men's reading room but the flame had been extinguished before any damage was caused.[174] This arson attempt was presumably carried out by members of the WSPU based in Birmingham or the wider Midlands, and both library incidents were possibly carried out by the same culprits. While arson was a popular tactic across the country and had been encouraged by Christabel Pankhurst,(for example, a house being built for Lloyd George in Surrey was badly damaged by arson in 1913, and in 1914 Hilda Burkitt, WSPU member formerly based in Birmingham, had been responsible for setting fire to a hotel in Felixstowe), the burning down of libraries seems unique to the Midlands as no other such cases have been recorded. Through these incidents the intention to shock was certainly achieved and the WSPU clearly demonstrated that its members were as capable of violence and carrying out destructive acts as men.

On the same night as the Carnegie Library fire suffragettes also planted a bomb at Moor Green Hall in King's Heath, the residence of the late Arthur Chamberlain (brother of Joseph), although it failed to detonate. The uninhabited house was being looked after by caretakers who found a piece of iron gas-piping about a foot long with one end connected by a fuse to a photographic lamp containing part of a candle. Explosive powder was found inside the pipe but the candle had gone out before any damage could be caused. Female footprints were found outside in the grounds of the building. A note left alongside the bomb read, 'Please post this to Mr McKenna, Home Office, London. Militancy is not dead, but if you are not you soon will be'.[175]

Early in March 1914 the *Birmingham Daily Post* published a letter to the editor from Catherine Osler, who was dismayed by the increase in militant outrages but also frustrated once more by the newspaper focus on those actions at the expense of the peaceful and law-abiding activities of her organisation:

SUFFRAGIST OUTRAGES, Sir, – In view of several acts of criminal destruction and attempted destruction recently perpetrated by 'militants' in this neighbourhood, the Birmingham Women's Suffrage Society desires once more to dissociate itself, as publicly and emphatically as possible, from all toleration of such outrages. It is well-nigh incredible that it should be needful for a society so long established, influential, and widely supported as our own to reiterate continually its abhorrence of a guerrilla warfare so wanton, futile, and certain to alienate sympathy from a noble cause. The necessity, alas, is due largely to the invariable practice of the press of advertising to the fullest extent every deplorable performance of the small band of lawbreakers, while it leaves unrecorded the legitimate and significant achievements of the main body of suffragists. The wonderful demonstration of February 14 at the Albert Hall received exactly one inch of space in the *Post*, with no mention whatever of the chief and novel feature of the vast gathering – viz., the assemblage of 300 to 400 delegates from men's associations and unions all over the kingdom, sent to demonstrate the sympathy and support of electors. C. C. Osler, President, Birmingham Women's Suffrage Society. March 9.

While the suffragists detested the behaviour of the militant suffragettes, they were also annoyed by frequently-made demands that they should prevent or stop the extreme tactics being employed by the WSPU. There was also an increasing sense of frustration that despite having campaigned in a legal and respectful manner for decades they were still being confused with the militants and being made to feel responsible for actions carried out by members of the WSPU. An article in *The Common Cause* in March asked, 'Why Do You Not Stop the Militants?' The simple answer given was: 'We do not "stop the Militants" because we cannot... The NUWSS has on more than one occasion appealed to the Women's Social and Political Union to abandon its disastrous tactics, and has repeatedly repudiated violence on its own behalf... But those to whom this tragic perversion of enthusiasm and courage and devotion into revenge and destruction is most of a heartbreak, are called upon to make their own protest against it not a negative but a positive one. We are often asked to stand aside altogether, as a protest, until militancy ceases. Such a course would be a betrayal.'[176]

Over the weekend of 13 March, less than a week after Catherine Osler's letter to the *Post*, a number of shocking incidents took place in Birmingham. Eight train carriages at Kings Norton train station were destroyed at a cost of £1,000. The *Birmingham Daily Mail* reported that detachments from the fire brigade were sent from King's Heath,

Cotteridge, Moseley Road, Northfield and the Central Station, such was the intensity of the blaze. It took two hours to extinguish as there was no nearby water supply, and 'so strongly did the fire burn that the blaze could be seen two miles away'.[177] A copy of *The Suffragette* newspaper was found nearby. The tennis pavilion at Olton Lawn Tennis club in Solihull was another victim of fire on the Friday evening. Here also a copy of *The Suffragette* was found, attached to some wire near the pavilion. The damage this time was estimated at £300. More dramatically, suffragettes had also decided to target St Philip's Cathedral in a daring act of vandalism. On Monday 16 March the *Birmingham Daily Post* reported the incident that had occurred on the Saturday. The extensive coverage justified Catherine Osler's exasperation at the attention given by the press to militant outrages:

MILITANTS' BUSY NIGHT.

SACRILEGE AT BIRMINGHAM CATHEDRAL.

INTERIOR DISFIGURED WITH WHITE PAINT.

'The militant suffragists of Birmingham have during the week-end added to their list of outrages by completely disfiguring the interior of the Cathedral Church of St Philip. In the past these misguided furies of the movement have discredited their cause in the city by many acts of wanton foolishness, but none has roused deeper execration, and done more to alienate public sympathy than will this latest act of vandalism.'

The article went on to describe how the culprits had covered the church interior with almost 20 separate painted inscriptions protesting against forcible feeding alongside more general calls for the vote. It was the latest development in the WSPU campaign that focused on getting church leaders to speak out against the Government policy of forcible feeding and the introduction of the 'Cat and Mouse Act'. A sense of the WSPU's sheer desperation is evident in the repetition of slogans urging 'Stop torturing English women in prison', 'Stop feeding by force. The Church has weight and influence'. 'Stop forcible feeding' was, according to the newspaper report, 'a cry that recurs with parrot-like persistency'. Other statements included 'Rise up ye people and see justice done', 'By giving the vote stop militancy', 'The Church can act', 'Give women their just right', 'The Church has a great responsibility towards women', 'The clergy must rise on our behalf', 'Give women justice', 'Stop torture', 'Give women the vote', 'The Church is responsible', 'Constitutional work is useless', 'Justice for women', and 'Women must rouse up the nation against forcible feeding if men will not'. A threat was also present: 'Be just to women before worse ---', the remaining words were indecipherable. The damage was carried out across the whole interior of the church, including the Edward Burne-Jones' stained glass windows.

The newspaper observed that 'it appears though they had worked hurriedly, and the large printed characters are like a first childish attempt at expression—as childish as the spite that prompted the deed'. As is typical of newspaper reporting of militant actions, there was no engagement with the demands of the women, but simply a patronising account of the incident that belittled the women and the cause they were fighting for.

The attack was, as the *Post* put it, an 'act of sacrilege', and it was 'believed the women painted their inscriptions for the benefit of the Judges, who were expected to attend the Cathedral yesterday on the eve of the Assizes, but their lordships do not arrive in the city until to-day. The outrage, it is said, may necessitate the closing of the Cathedral for several weeks'.[178] The report took pleasure in the fact that the women had been foiled in gaining the attention of the Judges. Moreover, the damage was quickly repaired and there is very little mention of the incident in the Cathedral minute books, apart from a news cutting related to a Cathedral Vestry meeting in April which only briefly mentioned the incident in order to announce that a donation of £10 had been made from 'ladies who did not sympathise with the outrage on that occasion'.[179] It is unclear what type of outrage these unidentified ladies might have sympathised with.

The militant action at Birmingham Cathedral was part of the wider WSPU campaign to target the Anglican Church. Services in the city had been disrupted since July 1913, coinciding with the introduction of the 'Cat and Mouse Act' earlier in the year. There was an expectation by women that the Church would play a moral leadership role and speak out against the brutal practice of forcible feeding of women. Deputations were sent to official residences and, if and when members were granted an audience, Church leaders were asked to condemn the Government's treatment of suffragette prisoners. *Votes for Women* published an article on 20 March that described a recent deputation to the Bishop of Manchester, asking for his support in agitating for the repeal of the Act. The Bishop defended the Government, remarking bizarrely that he could not advise it to abandon 'its only known method of protecting the subject against violence', and asking for a guarantee from the WSPU that they would cease acts of militancy. The Bishop of London had even made visits to Holloway Prison to investigate allegations of women being poisoned but he found no evidence and his statements referred to 'kindest possible spirit'. The WSPU saw this as a whitewash.

Some parts of the Church were supportive of women's enfranchisement, however. The Church League for Women's Suffrage had been founded in 1909 and, by 1914, had 5,000 members, both men and women. They supported the enfranchisement of women on the same terms as men and advocated constitutional methods. A Birmingham branch of this organisation operated from the home of Miss Griffiths on Harborne Road. But while some individual members of the Church were supporters of women's suffrage, that was made more difficult by methods of protest such as Cathedral vandalism. For example, in a letter to the *Birmingham Daily Post*, published on 17 March, the Reverend William Aidan Newman Hall of St Philip's Church in Dorridge wrote: 'As a suffragist of 20 years standing… such attacks on sacred buildings leave me no alternative but to withdraw my support from the movement to secure votes for women… when desecration of God's house is thought a fair and right means to secure a great moral reform, it behoves us to show practically the indignation we feel.'

A letter in response to Newman Hall appeared a couple of days later on 19 March, from a supporter of the campaign who had intimate knowledge of some of its members. Mr W. H. Ryland of Edgbaston wrote: 'Sir, – It is difficult to decide which of the so-called arguments against woman suffrage is the most illogical, but perhaps the palm may be awarded to the one put forward by Mr Newman Hall and others, which may be stated as follows: –"In principle I am in favour of woman suffrage, but owing to the violent actions of the militant suffragists, I have come to the conclusion that no woman ought to have the vote." The Conciliation Bill would have enfranchised, I believe, more than a million women. I don't know how many women have committed these violent actions – burning houses or other structures, defacing public buildings, breaking windows, destroying letters, etc. Perhaps there may be three or four hundred, but put the number at 500. Then 999,500 other women are to be deprived of the opportunity of voting because of the actions of these 500.' The author was William Henry Ryland, father of Bertha Ryland, WSPU militant and husband to Alice Ryland, subscriber to the BWSS along with her husband since the 1880s. William's sympathy with the women's plight is clear. Another commenter remarked in a letter to the *Birmingham Daily Mail* that 'the militant women are only copying men in their methods of fighting for their freedom… Sir Edward Carson and the Ulster militants are threatening far worse havoc, with the fire and sword of active rebellion, than anything yet attempted by the WSPU'. Like Catherine Osler, the author lay some of the blame at the door of the press, for focusing on militant activities at the expense of 'constitutional agitation'.[180]

Again the BWSS experienced public anger at militant tactics, which they officially condemned, although some of their members could understand their motivation. On 19 March at a well-attended meeting at Cotteridge Public Hall 'about a hundred youths, appeared to have attended with the sole object of creating a disturbance. Throughout the meeting they interrupted the speakers, despite the fact that the latter declared they were opposed to militancy. There was also a crowd outside the hall who amused themselves by banging tins and throwing stones on the roof. Miss S. M. Fry[181] said that their cause was unpopular because of the militants, but why should they be shocked at the militant methods, wrong though they were? Was there any section of the community which had not at some time or other used violence? This violence was merely a symptom of a disease affecting the country'.[182]

So who might have been responsible for the attack on the cathedral? Lilias Mitchell, sent by the WSPU leadership to Birmingham from Scotland in the summer of 1913, was arrested in the city in May under a charge of incitement to crime after a speech that she gave at Queen's College on 25 March implicated her in the cathedral incident. A news report described the proceedings:

'The remarks complained of, which formed the subject of the charge, were uttered at a meeting of the Women's Social and Political Union, held at Queen's College, Birmingham on March 25. Miss Mitchell presided at the meeting, and she was reported to have said, in opening the proceedings: – Birmingham within the last fortnight had increased its militancy, but not nearly enough; they must double and redouble it. "I am fully determined", Mitchell continued, "to do my utmost to increase the destruction of property in Birmingham, and I call upon every member to help me to do this". They had every justification for taking such a line of action, she considered. It was quite a simple thing, and it was very effective. Let them consider the result of the small messages which were left in the cathedral. The Pharisees and hypocrites poured letters into the papers about them, and were just like the Pharisees and hypocrites of the time of Christ. The protest in the cathedral was a protest against the desecration of the Church of God. They were firmly convinced that many of the leaders and members of the Christian Church to-day were degrading the Church, because they were tolerating the use of torture in our prisons. They were looking at the women's movement, which everyone knew was a great moral crusade, with apathy, and in doing so they were sinning against the Spirit of God, and, therefore, desecrating the Churches. It was a very mild militant protest which the women had made in the cathedral. "We could have burned that cathedral to the ground", the speaker went on, "but we did not do it this time." Notice the "this time". The Church was scorning to help the women's movement. The act to which this speech referred was the disfigurement of the interior of the Cathedral Church of St. Philip, which was discovered on Sunday, March 15.'[183]

In retaliation for the arrest of Mitchell, the grandstand at Castle Bromwich's racecourse was set on fire, described in the papers as 'the biggest act of arson in the

Birmingham district by the militant section of the suffragettes'.[184] In addition another serious fire occurred, this time in Harborne, which destroyed a large pavilion belonging to the Oratory Cricket Club. Nearby three messages had been left, each being printed in blue letters, that read 'Down with the Government that torture women', 'Down with sport and up with fair play for women', 'Enfranchisement of women will ensure safety of property'.[185] At her court hearing Lilias Mitchell refused to recognise the trial and asked why the Ulster militants were not receiving similar treatment from the Government. As well as general frustration with Asquith and the Government, the lenient treatment of Ulster militants was a source of irritation for the suffragettes: they saw that Irish Unionists were allowed to gather publicly where, unlike members of the WSPU on demonstrations, they did not face the same level of violence from police and members of the public that women frequently had to deal with. Indeed, the WSPU had been proscribed by the Metropolitan Police from holding public meetings in parks since April 1913, although the ban was frequently defied. After sentencing, Lilias went on hunger strike while in Winson Green but was released on licence under the 'Cat and Mouse Act' on 18 May. She was then reported to have been taken to a house in Hermitage Road, Edgbaston to recuperate – presumably this was the Ryland family home. Lilias and Bertha would probably have first met sometime in 1912, as they had both been imprisoned in Holloway that year for their part in the window-smashing campaign. As well as having the support of the sympathetic Ryland family to aid her convalescence, this time together would have given Lilias and Bertha the opportunity to plan more attacks.

While the reaction in the papers was to be expected, some incidents of violence occurred in the city that demonstrate an extreme reaction to the actions of the women. Moreover, the heavy emphasis on personal humiliation that was part of these attacks was arguably disproportionate to the WSPU attacks on property. The newspapers reported that on Sunday evening, 15 March, the day of the attack on the Cathedral, the WSPU office on John Bright Street had been vandalised: the window and door were covered in a mud-like substance, which turned out to be black paint mixed with acid, and a note was found that read 'We remember the park outrage. More will follow' and in Latin 'The law of revenge. It is right to derive instruction even from an enemy'. This possibly referred to the burning down of a kiosk in Cannon Hill Park at the beginning of March. Even more disturbingly, on 17 March the *Birmingham Gazette* published a letter from 'The Mysterious Fifty', the self-proclaimed culprits of the attack on the WSPU office, in which they described how else they planned to deal with these women.

Referred to as 'amusing' by the editor, it is anything but, as the group stated that 'we shall make them sorry for what they have done to Birmingham. We have succeeded in making bombs… we shall not be responsible for the safety of any person whom we know to be connected with these outrages and the cost to the damage of our Cathedral will be revenged twenty-fold'. They then describe their 'programme' which included total destruction of WSPU headquarters, personal disfigurement either by acid or cutting off their hair (easy by kidnapping), bomb for bomb, destruction of clothes by acid, binding and gagging after being rendered unconscious by fumes (better than prison), destruction of premises found harbouring them or their literature, tarring and feathering, branding of the face. The letter was signed 'We're Satisfied Prison's Useless'.

Retaliation against suffragettes continued and on 18 May an article in the *Courier*, a Dundee-based newspaper, reported an incident that had taken place somewhere in Birmingham: early on Saturday morning, the weekend of the burning down of the grandstand at Castle Bromwich and the cricket pavilion in Harborne, 'three young men, meeting in a suburb a woman who was carrying a can of tar and suffragette literature, approached her and asked if she was a suffragette. This being admitted the men tore off nearly all her clothing, saturated it with tar and set fire to it. They then decamped, leaving this girl to wander about until she obtained some clothing at a cottage'. In addition, a number of students had gone to the WSPU office in the city and smashed everything in there. These were, according to the *Courier*, 'drastic reprisals to the numerous outrages recently committed in Birmingham by the suffragettes'.

'I refuse to be tried'

Despite the risks involved in carrying out acts of militancy, such actions continued in the months leading up to summer 1914 and climaxed with a dramatic incident at the city's art gallery. At lunchtime on 9 June, almost exactly a year after the death of Emily Wilding Davison, who had died as a result of her injuries caused by an attempt to tie a WSPU scarf on to the King's horse at the Epsom Derby, Bertha Ryland walked into Birmingham Museum and Art Gallery. She approached the painting *John Bensley Thornhill (1773-1841) as a Boy* (known as *Master Thornhill*) by the well-known eighteenth-century artist George Romney and took a meat cleaver to it, slashing the canvas three times. The museum minutes recorded that 'the damage was committed by means of a chopper concealed beneath her jacket'.[186] It is unclear why she chose this particular painting but Bertha did have in her pocket a note explaining her actions:

Christ says "I came not to bring Peace but a Sword"

I attack this work of art deliberately as a protest against the Government's criminal injustice in denying women the vote, and also against the Government's brutal injustice in imprisoning, forcibly feeding, and drugging Suffragist militants, while allowing Ulster militants to go free.

Let all sensible men and women enquire into the cause of militancy instead of condemning the militants. We are militant because only so can the Vote be won; we need the Vote because only by it can the Women's Movement become a truly effective power. The Woman's Movement means the spiritual, mental and physical salvation of the race, because it is the one Movement that undertakes to stamp out sexual immorality and all its attendant horrors.

It is futile to attempt to crush this great Movement by persecution and misrepresentation. No power on earth can stop a Movement that is working, with Divine Guidance, for Purity and Righteousness.

BERTHA RYLAND [187]

The gallery was immediately closed, remaining so for a number of weeks, and damage to the painting was estimated at £50. In a number of letters sent to the local newspapers members of the public asked why it was necessary to keep the museum closed, one calling it 'a deplorable display of panic' and 'absolutely unwarranted' while suggesting that women should be the only ones barred from entry. [188]

Museum directors across the country were aware that their buildings and contents could be targeted by the WSPU at any time. Birmingham Museum's committee minutes from March 1914 reveal ongoing discussions about insuring works of art and arrangements had been made for the attendance of a detective officer at the building's entrance. There were also serious concerns that Emmeline Pankhurst might die as a result of her repeated hunger-striking, felt not just by her loyal WSPU members but also by the authorities, who feared the impact this could have. In April 1914 the Keeper of Birmingham Museum noted: 'I have made arrangements with the Detective Department and the editor of the *Birmingham Daily Mail* to kindly telephone me at once in the event of the decease of Mrs Pankhurst, and I think it would be advisable that the Gallery should be immediately closed in the event of her death.'[189]

This was not the first slashing incident that a member of the Birmingham WSPU had been involved with. The month before Bertha attacked the Romney painting, Maude Smith had been sent by the WSPU to the Royal Academy in London to target George Clausen's *Primavera*. One of the paintings of the year, causing damage to this particular work would garner even more attention. Maude described in her 1975 interview hiding a hatchet under her coat and, after arriving at the gallery, sitting in front of the painting for a long time, reluctant to take action but too scared to return to the WSPU office without fulfilling her mission.[190] The slashing of a painting was typically carried out by women on their own and would have presented a very different experience to smashing windows, which was usually done by small groups, or more clandestine activities like setting fire to pillar boxes or installing explosives. Once arrested, Maude gave the police a false name as she knew that conditions were better for new prisoners than for repeat offenders.

At Bertha Ryland's court hearing she, like Lilias Mitchell before her, reportedly exclaimed 'I refuse to have anything to do with the trial. I refuse to be tried'. She continually interrupted and was said to have responded to the prosecuting solicitor when asked about the damage to the painting: 'It is nothing to the damage caused by civil war. These Ulster militants are inciting to damage; why don't they arrest Sir Edward Carson and the rest of them?' Committed for trial and on remand in Winson Green, Bertha embarked on a hunger strike and was again forcibly fed. A few days later Bertha's father applied for bail, which was granted after Bertha gave a verbal undertaking that she would refrain from committing any similar act or attending suffragette meetings.[191] During that same week Lilias, now recovered from her prison ordeal, was re-arrested on 12 June after giving a speech at the Bull Ring to a huge crowd. Lilias urged her listeners to 'go on attacking property and persist in militancy to the end', should she be arrested again. At the hearing she refused to go back to prison: 'for over an hour the defendant kept up a fusillade of words' and had to be dragged out of the dock.[192] She was committed to prison for six months.

On the same day as Lilias' hearing another Birmingham WSPU member, Margaret Haly, was arrested for smashing the windows of the Labour Exchange in Corporation Street with a hammer, in protest against the forcible feeding of Bertha Ryland. She was committed for two months with hard labour. All three women would have been in Winson Green at the same time, from 12-15 June, before Bertha was given bail. Lilias was then released a few days later after hunger-striking and went to a house in Edgbaston to recuperate, again probably at Bertha's family home. It was reported, however, at the beginning of July, that Lilias had fled the city, days after she should have presented herself to the court for re-imprisonment under the 'Cat and Mouse Act'. At the same time as Bertha and Lilias were in court, Hilda Burkitt, our suffragette protester from the Bingley Hall meeting in 1909, was in court in Felixstowe for setting fire to a hotel, for which she would receive two years with hard labour. After her stint in Holloway in 1912 for window-smashing, Hilda had spent the following two years moving around the country carrying out militant actions and evading the police, a lifestyle common to many of the more militant WSPU members.

In July a statement by Bertha Ryland was published in *The Suffragette*. Here it was revealed that she had suffered a kidney complaint since 1912, the year she was first convicted for her part in the window-smashing campaign, and that forcible feeding should never have been performed as this had drastically worsened her condition. Bertha's testimonial is a harrowing and heart-breaking one: 'I resisted, and was seized round the waist by wardresses, and once tied round the waist in the operating chair. This mauling of the unprotected kidney together with the retching and choking, strained and twisted the kidney and caused chronic inflammation.' The article provides further details on how the condition had caused her almost continuous pain, which makes her work for the WSPU at this time, organising meetings and events all over the region, all the more remarkable. Bertha also described how she was restrained by four wardresses while the prison doctor, Dr Ahern, forced a thick rubber tube into her nostril and down her throat, 'the acute agony, the inevitable retching, and choking, and the feeling of suffocation, accompanied by the utter helplessness, all combined to make this the most unutterably hideous experience'. The treatment had a marked effect on her mental state: 'I lay in bed practically all the time... feeling too ill and exhausted to do anything. In addition to this feeling of exhaustion there came long periods of mental depression... Besides an unaccountable feeling of misery and depression, my memory seemed to be going, and it was a great effort to think clearly, or fix my attention on anything... the mental anguish caused by forcible feeding is, of course, quite indescribable.'[193] On 17 July the *Birmingham Daily Post* reported that the trial had been postponed due to concerns about Bertha's health.

Bertha's trial had not taken place by the time war broke out in August 1914, after which all imprisoned suffragettes were granted amnesty. The charges against her were officially dropped in September 1914. In a letter sent to the Home Office dated 25 September, J. Ernest Hill, Prosecuting Solicitor for the city of Birmingham, suggested that Bertha was responsible for her actions but had probably been in 'an hysterical condition which might possibly have made her more than ordinarily liable to do such an act of damage'. He revealed that Bertha was now recovering from an operation but suggested that she would be willing to apologise and that if the case was withdrawn he would ensure that she made some reparation to the city for the damage caused.[194] A matter of months after the painting attack, the museum minutes record that *Master Thornhill* had been fully repaired and would be placed back on display as soon as glass could be procured.[195] The following year the committee reported that Bertha's mother, Alice, had donated two paintings to the museum, presumably part of the agreed reparations offered in exchange for the dismissal of Bertha's trial.[196] *Master Thornhill* is now part of the collection of the Museum of Fine Arts in Boston (it was on loan to Birmingham at the time of Bertha's attack).

One final militant action occurred in Birmingham before the outbreak of war on 4 August: the burning down of a house in Yardley on 23 July. The accompanying note protested against forcible feeding and urged the release of suffragette prisoners. Two weeks later Britain declared war on Germany. Only days afterwards, the WSPU, in a dramatic turnaround, suspended all activity in order to support the war effort. Two years of intense militant action, and the subsequent violence by and against the women, were now at an end. How much it had achieved is debatable. The Reform Bill of 1913 showed that there was some appetite for change, as did Asquith's positive reaction to the NUWSS Pilgrimage, but increasingly extreme militant actions, while popular on the front pages of newspapers, continued to be condemned by most politicians and the wider public. It was also having a catastrophic effect on the women themselves, made to repeatedly endure forcible feeding and being constantly hounded by the police, and, at this point in 1914, 'many of the more militant members of the campaign already believed themselves to be at war'.[197] However, this new armed war between empires symbolised, for suffrage campaigners, all that was wrong with having only men enfranchised and in power. Furthermore, not only would women still have to tolerate their voices being ignored but they would also be expected to contribute to the war effort. While for some the fight for enfranchisement would have to be suspended for the moment, for others the war would afford women the opportunity to pressure politicians into recognising their strengths and abilities, thereby making it impossible for them *not* to give women the vote.

Aftermath: 1914-1918

'Repression cannot break the spirit of liberty'

The Common Cause, 28 August 1914

War

Three days after Britain declared war against Germany the NUWSS newspaper, *The Common Cause*, published an article titled 'What War Means'.[198] At a meeting of the International Suffrage Alliance in London that week, concerns had been expressed that women's voices would not be heard as the country entered into conflict. All present were of the opinion that the consequences of going to war would be dire, asserting 'that women have an equal right with men to speak and to be heard' on this grave matter. The national organisation passed a resolution, urging a peaceful solution be found before too many lives were lost, noting that there was a strong anti-war feeling within women but especially amongst working-class women who knew that they would be hardest hit. Towards the end of the month the NUWSS stated that it was temporarily suspending its ordinary political work but assured members that it was doing a good deal of extraordinary political work with excellent results, as 'Suffragists do not change their minds, or lower their flag'.[199] The potential part that the National Union could play and its activities at the outbreak of war 'provide striking evidence of the centrality of the role that the non-militant women's suffrage societies played in the lives of their members by this time, and of the extent and efficiency of its network'.[200]

In Birmingham, although campaigning was officially suspended, the BWSS continued to attract new supporters, reporting 246 new members in the year 1914-15, giving a total membership of 955. Fees were now being put towards the war effort and the annual report noted that 'it is gratifying to record that in spite of the war the bulk of our subscribers have paid their subscriptions as usual, thus enabling the Society to keep open its Office and to undertake and organise a great deal of war relief work that would otherwise have been impossible'.[201] Non-subscribing members also continued to rise and there were now 4,640 Friends of Women's Suffrage. In the survey of that first year of war the BWSS also observed: 'In spite of the suspension of political work, the last eight months have constituted one of the most active and important epochs in the whole history of the National Union. It is quite possible that none of its most impressive achievements in the past – neither the London procession of 1910, nor the Pilgrimage of 1913 – have produced an effect on public opinion as has the demonstration of public spirit and patriotic service by Suffragists in this crisis of our country's history. Their readiness and capacity to cope with the numerous and difficult problems which have developed on all sides, have caused their help and guidance to be sought by many who are opposed to the principle of women's suffrage: and the very ministers and politicians who would refuse women recognition as citizens have been glad to avail themselves of their advice and experience.'[202] Even at this early stage of the conflict with Germany, long-serving suffrage campaigners could see the opportunity that presented itself, that politicians would have to acknowledge the contribution that women were making.

Similarly concerned that women's voices would be ignored, the WSPU leadership firmly laid the blame for the outbreak of war at the feet of male politicians. In an article by Christabel Pankhurst titled 'The War', published in *The Suffragette* on 7 August, she observed: 'This then is the World as men have made it, life as men had ordered it. A man-made civilisation, hideous and cruel enough in time of peace, is to be destroyed… this great war, whether it comes now, or by some miracle is deferred till later, is Nature's vengeance – is God's vengeance upon the people who held women in subjection, and by doing that have destroyed the perfect human balance.' She went further, asserting: 'Had women been equal partners with men from the beginning, human civilisation would have been wholly different from what it is. The whole march of humanity would have been to a point other than we have reached at this moment of horrible calamity… In the coming days it is the enfranchised women – for women must and will be enfranchised – who will save the race.' The Pankhursts clearly recognised the potential opportunities that war could present to women and, in a dramatic and shrewd change of direction, they now began to work with their previously sworn enemy, the Liberal politicians, many of whom had repeatedly thwarted attempts to win the vote for women in the years leading up to 1914 and had controversially introduced forcible feeding and the 'Cat and Mouse Act' in order to deal with hunger-striking women. After war was declared the WSPU ceased all militant activity and its organisers were dismissed. As the conflict began to rage, Emmeline and Christabel 'became patriotic feminists, supporting their country in its hour of need and urging all suffragettes of the WSPU to do likewise… [they] encouraged women to engage in war work, believing that the eventual reward for such loyalty would be the parliamentary vote'.[203]

In terms of local WSPU organisation it is difficult to trace the immediate impact that the cessation of campaigning had: 'The deliberate rejection by Emmeline and Christabel Pankhurst of a democratic constitution makes it as hard to see just what actions were taken by WSPU branches throughout the country on the outbreak of war as it had made it to see anything before the war but the smoke of the arson campaign.'[204] Changes to the lives of individual campaigners can be traced, however. As we know, in August 1914, Bertha Ryland was recovering at home from her most recent ordeal in prison; her trial would be cancelled in October. The Ryland family continued to donate money to the BWSS, something they had done on a regular basis since the 1880s, even during their involvement with the WSPU. A Miss Ryland is recorded as having worked for the Birmingham Lady Mayoress's depot from May 1916 to April 1917. This organisation was set up by Mrs Martineau, the Lady Mayoress, in 1914, to help receive and distribute clothing for wounded soldiers and troops and to dispatch parcels to prisoners of war in Germany. It is difficult to know if this is Bertha Ryland or her sister Edith. Although she suffered permanent kidney problems as a result of forcible feeding, Bertha lived until the 1970s.

At the outbreak of war, Maude Smith was in Holloway Gaol, sentenced to six months for slashing the George Clausen painting at the Royal Academy, and was undergoing forcible feeding. After release she went to convalesce with WSPU colleagues in London. At some point after her involvement with the WSPU ceased, Maude moved to Shropshire where she was housekeeper for a family friend. She later moved back to Birmingham and died in Erdington in June 1977.

Lilias Mitchell did not return to Birmingham after she absconded before her trial in July 1914. She remained undetected, her case dismissed as part of the amnesty after the war began. She later worked as a secretary for the YWCA and as a social worker in Edinburgh, actively promoting prison reform. Her death was announced in *The Scotsman* on 25 September 1940, where she was described as 'a woman of keen intellect, wide culture, and boundless enthusiasm'.

Hilda Burkitt was released from Holloway Gaol on 8 August. An article in *The Suffragette* published on 7 August reported on her condition: 'She is quite alone, and is being forcibly fed four times a day. She is sick after every feeding. She has lost over a stone in weight. She suffers agonies with her nerves, and her throat is in a terrible condition… Miss Burkitt has now been forcibly fed over two hundred and fifty times.' Hilda had petitioned the Home Office on 6 August for release; the document reveals a sense of defeat and an awareness that she had gone as far as she could. In the petition she states: 'After a great deal of thought and consideration I have made up my mind that, in future I shall do no more militant work so if you can see your way clear to order my release from prison at once, I will undertake not to commit any more criminal actions.

I have been in prison since April 28th, and have been forcibly fed during the whole time, 292 times so far, but it is not because of this I am petitioning it is because I wish to lead a peaceful life in the future.'[205] A handwritten note at the bottom of the daily prison report recording her release states that she was taken to Euston Station and was heading for Birmingham to the care of her father.[206] In the summer of 1916 Hilda Burkitt married Leonard Mitchener and the couple settled in Lancashire. Hilda died in Morecambe in March 1955.

Nellie Hall, another Birmingham WSPU member, was also mentioned in *The Suffragette* article of 7 August. She was said to be 'suffering from [a] very sore throat, and from pains in her ears and eyes. At times she is seized with partial blindness; she cannot see anything then, and cannot read. She is losing weight. She is rather quiet and does not say very much… She was allowed no book during those ten days, and was fed on the floor most of the time'. Nellie had moved to London but returned to Birmingham after her release from prison. She then joined the Post Office and became the first mail sorter for the British Expeditionary Force.[207] Despite her treatment at the hands of the Government, Nellie was desperately keen to offer her services to the country at the outbreak of war, even writing to the city's recruiting office in the hope that she could be permitted to join the army. She received a reply in November 1914 rejecting her offer but advising that 'if you wish to assist, I would suggest you should persuade any man you know who is eligible, to do his duty by enlisting at once, if all women would act as Recruiting Sergeants in this manner no doubt we should soon obtain all the men required and there would be no fear of invasion of this Country'.[208] In 1920 Nellie was married and moved to Warwickshire. In 1928 she became secretary to Emmeline Pankhurst. Following Pankhurst's death, Nellie and her family emigrated to Canada.

Votes for Women also blamed men for the conflict but saw equality between the sexes as the solution: 'This awful indescribable ruin is the supreme result of a human world ordered and managed and governed by men alone, a world in which women are only permitted to fill subordinate and unimportant positions… They know full well that it is because of the one-sidedness of a solely male Government that it has come to grief, and that a solely female Government would fall upon equal disaster. They demand, therefore, not domination, but equality.'[209] In the issue for 21 August, Emmeline and Frederick Pethick Lawrence announced that *Votes for Women* was now the official paper of the United Suffragists, a group that they had recently joined. The United Suffragists had been established earlier that year by former WSPU members and non-militant suffragists in response to increased militancy and the organisation admitted both men and women. Unlike the WSPU and NUWSS, the United Suffragists continued to campaign for women's votes as the war progressed. Along with enfranchising women, they also campaigned for compensation for women whose husbands had been killed in the war, equal pay for women workers, and for women to have a say in any peace settlement or post-war rebuilding.

The right to serve

In early 1915 inadequate munitions production in Britain meant that troops on the front line were facing mass shortages. A Board of Trade circular was issued in March, inviting women to register themselves for 'war service' due to the shortage of labour. This was viewed positively by campaigners attached to the United Suffragists who commented in *Votes for Women*: 'We heartily congratulate the Government upon having at last woke up to the fact that women have services to give… besides the enormous number of women doing national service by looking after their homes, there are nearly six million women at regular work in organized trades, whose service may truly be described as national.' But problems that might occur once men returned from war, potentially now finding themselves unemployed, or for women workers forced out of their new roles, along with the impact that could arise from upper-class women accepting work for low wages, were quickly identified by the United Suffragists: 'All women who register for employment upon the work of men must refuse to accept a penny less wages than the man was receiving.' They also recognised the contribution that women made to the war effort as a bargaining chip. The article urged women to 'demand political enfranchisement… if women are capable of "war service", if they are to be inscribed on the national "roll of honour", it is not only shamefully unjust, it is increasingly ridiculous that they should be penalised by disenfranchisement and dishonoured by inequality'.[210] The shortage of munitions also presented an opportunity to the Pankhursts, which they were ready to seize. Emmeline Pankhurst, in collaboration with David Lloyd George, now Minister for Munitions, organised a women's march, demanding the 'right to serve' in the war effort. The demonstration took place in London on 17 July with around 20,000 women in attendance; the cost of the march was funded by Lloyd George and the Government.

In Birmingham, although the WSPU had disbanded, suffrage campaigning was continued by the United Suffragists. A Birmingham branch was formed in February 1915, led initially by Bertha Brewster, a member of the executive committee of the national organisation. A former member of the WSPU, Bertha had served time in prison in 1911 for window-smashing and had famously written a letter to the *Daily Telegraph* in 1913:

Sir,

Everyone seems to agree upon the necessity of putting a stop to Suffragist outrages; but no one seems certain how to do so. There are two, and only two, ways in which this can be done. Both will be effectual.

1. Kill every woman in the United Kingdom.

2. Give women the vote.

Yours truly,

Bertha Brewster

The Honorary Secretary and organiser in Birmingham was Margaret Haly, former WSPU window-smasher, who had been arrested and imprisoned in Winson Green in June 1914. In her first report on the branch activities, Haly observed that 'members who were in doubt as to whether or not it would be wiser to drop Suffrage now will be reassured by the sympathy with which the work of the branch met during its first week. The meeting at Queen's College on February 11 showed a very real appreciation of the importance of keeping the Suffrage flag flying'. The demand for copies of *Votes for Women* was reported to have outstripped supply and more copies were urgently ordered.[211] Other Birmingham WSPU members were also involved in the organisation: former branch organiser Dorothy Evans, at that time working at Anstey College, Erdington, chaired a meeting in March 1915 and 'received a delighted welcome from her old comrades in the "great cause"'.[212] And in July 1915 an 'At Home' was held by Bertha Ryland's mother at the family home at 19 Hermitage Road in Edgbaston. However, some suffragettes and suffragists were vehemently against the war. In her 1975 interview, Maude Smith stated that she was a pacifist and so, because of her views, refused to help the war effort, something that caused conflict with some of her former militant colleagues.[213] After resigning from her position as United Suffragist organiser in July 1915, Margaret Haly actively campaigned against the war throughout 1916 and 1917. On Christmas Eve 1916 she addressed a peace meeting at the Bull Ring, in early 1916 she gave lectures to United Suffragist members on the international situation, and in July 1917 Haly organised a peace meeting on behalf of the Women's International League (established by former NUWSS members) and the Fellowship of Reconciliation, formed in 1914 in protest at the war, held in the Bull Ring as part of the Women's Peace Crusade.[214] On this evening 300 people marched from Old Street to the Bull Ring to protest their anger at the seemingly never-ending conflict with Germany.

Towards the end of 1915, questions started to be asked 'regarding the disenfranchisement of soldiers who lost their votes because of residency requirements that necessitated a stable domicile'.[215] Moreover, a large number of soldiers would not have been eligible to vote anyway, as they did not fulfil the property qualification. This now signalled a chance for suffrage campaigners. A resolution was proposed and carried at a United Suffragists meeting in Birmingham: 'That in view of the likelihood of attempts being made to extend the parliamentary franchise for men before the next General Election, this meeting declares its determination to oppose any readjustment or increase of the franchise which does not include equality of franchise rights for women.'[216] Perhaps there was now a real glimmer of hope on the horizon. However, as the war progressed, disagreements emerged within the NUWSS, which came to a head in 1915 and threatened the organisation. Some members of the executive committee wanted to join a women's peace conference, planned to take place at The Hague in April that year, which would bring together women from across Europe, including from Germany. Millicent Fawcett was entirely opposed to the idea, stating that 'it would hardly be possible to bring together women of the belligerent countries without violent bursts of anger and mutual recrimination'.[217] A meeting of the National Council in February highlighted the emerging split between those who were against the war and those who supported it and there were resignations from the executive committee.

A Special Council Meeting was called, to take place on 17 and 18 June in Birmingham at the Midland Institute, where an attempt at reconciliation would be made and new members elected to the executive, although this arguably 'completed the rout of democratic suffragists and put an end to wide geographic representation as well as to any significant political diversity'.[218] One of those from outside London to be elected to the committee was Catherine Osler. Most of the regional societies backed Fawcett, although 'a strong argument held by many in personal sympathy with the peace propaganda advocates was that whatever might be the right course for individuals to pursue, the Union, as a corporate body, should steer clear of campaigning on divisive topics – and on ones for which it was not specifically formed'.[219] Despite these difficulties the organisation did manage to come to an agreement about the proposed extension of the franchise. The *Birmingham Daily Gazette* reported on 19 June that at the meeting a resolution had been put forward by the Birmingham Society: 'That this Council of the NUWSS, noting the promise of the Prime Minister to consider the extension of the franchise to soldiers and sailors, in recognition for their patriotic services during the war, urges that the same recognition should be extended for widely-acknowledged patriotic services rendered by women.'

A partial victory

Although not actively campaigning, both Fawcett and Pankhurst met with politicians during the war as the discussions around electoral changes developed. In August 1916 a deputation led by Fawcett met with cabinet members Andrew Bonar Law and Lord Cecil. The *Staffordshire Advertiser* reported on the proceedings. The sense of urgency, that the suffragists must force the issue and keep pressure on the politicians, is clear: in the meeting, Fawcett warned that 'in the event of legislation, which would in any degree alter the existing basis of the franchise, women suffragists would no longer be content to stand aside'. Lord Cecil stated that 'he himself would not assent to any alteration in the franchise or in registration which substantially increased the number of votes unless it included some measure of enfranchisement for women'. In a letter to Asquith, Fawcett had warned that if the number of male voters increased but women were still excluded, 'the injustice of such exclusion – always great and for long keenly felt – will become more intolerable than ever after the war, when the problem of men's and women's labour has to be faced… the discovery by their employers of the great value of their labour, may possibly produce an apparent clashing of interests between the sexes… If a new qualification is to be established based on services in the war, then the claim of women to share in such a qualification cannot be ignored'. This was a claim not just by women who had worked in the factories but by those women who had lost husbands or sons.[220] The letter was signed by a number of organisations, including Bertha Brewster on behalf of the United Suffragists.

War, and women's role within it, forced politicians to recognise the contribution made by women and raised an absurd situation whereby the Government, on the one hand, encouraged women to support the war effort through any means necessary, but, on the other, prevented them from having any democratic power. This was clearly no longer tenable. However, not all former suffragettes felt the same way. Indeed, the reaction of Emmeline and Christabel Pankhurst was particularly extreme, as they 'burnished [their] patriotic credentials by refusing to endorse a female vote until the soldier's vote was secured first'.[221] This must have felt like a betrayal for some WSPU members after all they had gone through, and especially for women like Maude Smith and Margaret Haly, both unbending in their pacifism. As the year progressed the political situation was one of turmoil. Military setbacks at the Dardanelles and the Somme had led to the threat of a Conservative backbench rebellion and Asquith was forced to resign in December 1916. He was succeeded by David Lloyd George.

In early 1917 a White Paper on electoral reform was published. This proposed almost complete adult suffrage for men but also crucially included a clause on women's votes which, if successful, would give around six million women the vote, about half the number of eligible male voters. The NUWSS, although not completely satisfied, was happy to accept the deal being offered. On 7 March a suffrage demonstration was held at the Midland Institute, with Catherine Osler presiding and Millicent Fawcett in attendance. It was reported later that the Society had 'decided to support the Electoral Reform Bill as recommended by the Speaker's Conference, since, though it did not confer on women equal political rights with men, it seemed to afford 'the best immediate opportunity of obtaining votes for women on the most favourable terms practicable for the time being'. The report continued, the Bill 'confers what is practically manhood suffrage, on a six months' residential qualification; and gives an unequal but very substantial enfranchisement to women (a) on the basis of the Municipal Register as householders, (b) as wives of male voters, (c) as University graduates'.[222]

It had been decided that the qualifying age for women would be fixed at 30, thereby preventing the number of female voters outnumbering that of male voters, something that politicians were keen to avoid, although this aim was not explicitly stated. There was also a fear that younger women would be more prone to radicalism and it was felt that women who were older and potentially married with children would be more able to understand the intricacies of politics. The number of women who would become eligible to vote represented approximately 40% of the total population of women in the UK. The age restriction was the part of the Bill that disappointed suffrage campaigners the most and was criticised by the United Suffragists for potentially excluding many women war workers and young widows. The BWSS, while acknowledging that the compromise was 'illogical, partial, unequal in incidence, and open to many objections', felt that there were reasons to be hopeful, as the enfranchisement of at least some women 'decisively breaks down the barrier of sex and leaves the way open for future rectification and readjustment. It places about six millions of women (to eleven millions of men) on the Register, and if passed into law this year, will enable the women of the nation to make their needs and claims understood and considered in the reconstruction, social and industrial, which must follow the War'.[223]

For Osler and the BWSS the reasons for this change were clear. It was 'no doubt, the wider opportunity afforded to women by the War to prove conclusively that their active and patriotic service and devotion to their country and their kind is in no way less valuable or less essential than that of men; but also the demonstration that the removal of the artificial restrictions on women's talents and activities will, as Suffragists have always maintained, materially augment the effective power and prosperity of the country'.[224] While the narrative of women being somehow 'rewarded' for their work during the war has been presented, not least by the suffrage organisations themselves, it is clear that the Government had no other option but to extend the franchise and could not legitimately continue to deny women a democratic say in the country's future. One of the terrible ironies was that if the law was passed it would exclude women like the 22-year-old Nellie Hall, desperate to serve her country, but who would not be eligible to vote until she came of age.

On 19 June 1917 the House of Commons voted by 385 to 55 in favour of the women's clause in the Representation of the People Bill. Women over thirty who were householders, wives of householders, occupiers of property of £5 or more annual value, or University graduates, could now vote. At the annual meeting of the BWSS held on 29 June 1917, reported in the *Birmingham Daily Post* the next day, the Reform Bill was the central focus, although there was a clear sense that the victory was a partial one and that the vote was only one part of a wider social justice campaign to improve the lives of women. After all her battles with the newspapers, feeling almost constant frustration at their sensationalising of militant incidents at the expense of constitutional and educational suffragist activity, Osler remarked that the 'conversion of the press was particularly significant' but warned that they must not allow this to sway them from the matter at hand: 'Notwithstanding the encouragement they had received there must be no unbuckling of their armour or of laying down the peaceful sword of their spirit.' She called for the work of the Society to continue, as they 'stood for a good deal more than the actual demand for the vote. They stood as the protectors and watchful guardians of women's interests in the very widest sense... The suffrage societies would still be needed as a channel of communication and information, of sympathy and support between the women voters and the workers who were not enfranchised'.[225]

The Representation of the People Act finally received Royal Assent on 6 February 1918. The last edition of *Votes for Women* was published that month. In the leading article titled 'The Future', the United Suffragists executive committee surmised: 'We do not know what the future will contain for the new men and women voters. Of one thing only are we certain, that peace must come some day. There is a whole civilisation to be healed, a whole new world to be built up. Looking back over the years, seeing the magnificent sacrifices that have been offered up in the cause of women's freedom, we have no fears as to the use that will be made by women of their votes, working side by side with the men whose citizenship they now share.' The organisation also looked back to the wider campaign: 'We realise to the full how much to-day's victory is the outcome of the struggle and sacrifice of the militant years 1905-1914, and of the women's steady and educational campaign that dates back to 1867, and, indeed, of every bid for freedom that has been made by woman all down the ages.'[226]

In light of the new political landscape, in 1918, after 50 years of campaigning, the BWSS ceased to exist and merged with the local branch of the National Union of Women Workers, resulting in the formation of the Birmingham Society for Equal Citizenship, with Catherine Osler as its President.[227] In March 1918 the *Women Workers, Quarterly Magazine of the Birmingham Branch of the National Union of Women Workers* included an article by Osler. Titled 'At Last!' she reflected on the campaign prior to the outbreak of war. While it was certainly an achievement to be celebrated, the conditions of qualifying were 'not all that could be desired – far from it! They do not fulfil the original and unaltered demand of suffragists for "the vote on the same terms as it is or may be granted to men". It leaves still unrepresented classes of women who are among the worthiest, most indispensable workers for their country and for their fellows'. Osler also considered the wider campaign and the sacrifices that many women had made: 'Some, indeed, have dared infinitely more than this – have courted and endured gross insult, maltreatment, torture, death itself, in the determination to draw the world's attention to women's wrongs... the startling campaign of the militant section... has now become as a nightmare memory, but one which will survive in history.' She also acknowledged the campaign's well-established roots, going back to the 1860s, stating that 'it was not because on grounds of reason and common sense suffrage was "bound to come" but because the nation had for 50 years been patiently and unceasingly educated to the conviction of its justice and righteousness, that the conditions of war enabled its advocates to make the final effort which brought victory... a great dividing barrier has disappeared from the ranks of women themselves, and that henceforth we may go forward shoulder to shoulder'.[228]

Christabel Pankhurst and Smethwick

In 1917, after disbanding the WSPU, Emmeline and Christabel Pankhurst formed the Women's Party. This new organisation would represent their political views, which now conflated the winning of the war with the women's cause. Emmeline explained that women needed a party of their own because 'men had grown so accustomed to managing the world in the past that it had become rather difficult for women in politics to hold their own if they were associated with men'.[229] However, the Pankhursts went much further than other women's organisations in their patriotism and anti-German feeling, indeed, 'the lynchpin of the suffragette's self-fashioning during the Great War was to repeatedly draw attention to the loyalty, bravery, and hard-headed militancy of disenfranchised women, in comparison to the cosmopolitanism, pacifism, and socialism of a host of men, such as Liberals, union men, or conscientious objectors, who were enfranchised only because of their sex'.[230] In a speech given at Birmingham's Town Hall in February 1918, Christabel declared that 'women would use the vote for the crushing of the enemy, and to bring about victory for the Allied cause'. She also singled out certain groups for particular criticism, stating that 'it was not true that Britain wanted peace. The only people who wanted peace were the shirkers who had gone into the munitions factories in order to save their skins'. At the meeting she passed a resolution to support the Government's proposals to remove exemptions from men in protected occupations, declaring that 'eligible men hitherto exempt from military service shall take their place in the fighting ranks'. Heckled by pacifist protesters, Christabel retorted: 'We all want peace with victory, which is the only way to have peace with honour. We will have no peace until the German fiends and beasts are crushed.'[231] Her startling rhetoric contrasts starkly with the pacifism of former colleagues such as Margaret Haly, although Christabel's propagandist views were 'closely aligned to those found in the contemporary mainstream press'.[232]

Later in the year, less than a fortnight after the war had ended, a Bill was rushed through Parliament which allowed women to stand for election to Parliament on equal terms with men, 'ironically allowing those women aged between twenty-one and thirty years to stand for a parliament they could not elect'.[233] Emmeline declined the chance to run for election in favour of her daughter and eventually it was decided that Christabel would attempt to become Member of Parliament for the new industrial working-class constituency of Smethwick. She was originally going to stand for the seat at Westbury in Wiltshire, perceived as a safer seat, but instead she later decided to run in Smethwick. While their views had become increasingly jingoistic as the war progressed, and their political tendencies leaned far more towards the right than before, the Women's Party also 'advocated equal pay for equal work, equal marriage and divorce laws, equality of parental rights, the raising of the age of consent, equal opportunity of employment, and equality of rights and responsibilities in regard to the social and political service of the nation'.[234] Emmeline and Christabel's patriotism had advantages, however: 'The Women's Party grafted a progressive feminist agenda onto the patriotic tree that had served the WSPU so well in their wartime quest for the vote.'[235]

Christabel Pankhurst's attempt to be elected to Parliament was backed by Lloyd George, and she was given a 'coupon' or letter of approval from him in order to increase her chances of success. She pledged 'to secure a lasting peace based on material guarantees against future German aggression and, second, to improve the social conditions of the working classes through a levelling up of society, by social reform, industrial salvation and wealth production'.[236] Influential on her decision to stand for this particular seat, Smethwick had over 12,000 women voters on the electoral register, now administered by local authorities in preparation for the election. On 14 December, the day before the election, referred to as the 'khaki' election, *The Times* was convinced that Christabel would win. Although it did put her selection for the seat down to 'male chivalry' (Major Thompson, the Coalition candidate, had been persuaded by Lloyd George to step aside in favour of Christabel), the paper observed that Christabel 'has made steady progress, and though she has been subjected to organised heckling, it has been child's play compared with what she had to face in her militant days. Local opinion regards the results of tomorrow's poll as a foregone conclusion'. In the end, Christabel lost to her Labour Party opponent but by a small margin of only 775 votes. The loss has been put down to the unequal franchise – no young Smethwick women were able to vote for Christabel, who was 'wildly popular among a set of patriotic, independent munitions girls', plus there was a low turnout across the country (less than 55%), perhaps unsurprising given that war had ended only a month before.[237]

The Times also covered Mary Macarthur's campaign to become Labour MP for the newly-created constituency of Stourbridge (Macarthur had founded the National Federation of Women Workers in 1906 and had famously led the Cradley Heath chain makers strike of 1910). Although both Mary Macarthur and Christabel Pankhurst had previously been on the same side, fighting for women's rights, Mary now actively campaigned against Christabel, visiting Smethwick to support her fellow Labour candidate. Given her campaigning and trade union experience, Mary was also widely viewed as favourite to win her seat. A NUWSS candidate also ran for a West Midlands constituency: Margery Corbett Ashby, a member of the NUWSS executive, ran as a Liberal candidate for Birmingham Ladywood. Sadly both women lost: Macarthur to the Liberal candidate, John William Wilson, while Corbett Ashby had chosen to run against the Unionist Neville Chamberlain for the Birmingham Ladywood constituency, which he won with 69% of the vote while Corbett Ashby came third with only 11.5% of the share. The turnout there was only 40%. Some blamed Mary Macarthur's defeat on her being forced to put her married name of Mrs Anderson on the ballot paper.[238] However, both women were up against well-established and experienced politicians so the losses perhaps should not be surprising, and although Macarthur came second to Wilson, her respectable 32.7% share of the vote compared favourably to Wilson's result of 38.5%, an even more impressive outcome given the short amount of time women candidates had to prepare for the election. While the war clearly affected the election, the experiences of the three women indicate that there was still much work to be done in encouraging the wider population to vote for women. Indeed, the BWSS annual report remarked that 'evidence was only too forthcoming of indifference and ignorance among voters; and the need for awakening their sense of responsibility all over the country was emphasised by the whole Election'.[239]

Women who had been involved in the campaign for women's votes now began to be recognised for their contribution to social, civic and political causes. In July 1919 the University of Birmingham presented an honorary degree to ten citizens, including Catherine Osler. In presenting her for the Master's Degree, Sir Oliver Lodge, Principal of the University and a long-time supporter of women's suffrage, said: 'All those who have worked for the public service of women must rejoice at the vital help they have afforded to the country in its need, and at the universal recognition now given to their labours. As a great modern University, in which women take equal rank with men, we delight to associate with us one who has devoted her life to furthering the moral, intellectual, and social welfare of her sex.'[240] In further recognition of her contribution, a portrait of Osler by Edward Harper was funded by a testimonial presented to her by the NUWSS (the painting is now in the collection of Birmingham City Council). The money left over, along with a donation from the Osler family, was used to help women BA students obtain their MA.[241] Osler announced her retirement from the Society the following year. In the BWSS report for 1919-20, her outstanding work on behalf of the Society was acknowledged: 'Words are inadequate to express all that the Society owes to its President for twenty years, Mrs Alfred C. Osler. Only those who have worked with and under her can justly appreciate the patience, wisdom, courage, and unselfish devotion she has put into the work for the cause of the enfranchisement of women, and for the general raising of the standard and welfare of all womanhood. It has been a great life work, and one moreover which has been triumphantly crowned with success.'[242]

In 1924 Catherine Osler died at the age of 70 after a short illness. Her impact on the movement was widely recognised and she was remembered by the *Birmingham Gazette*: 'Mrs. Osler threw herself into the movement for women's enfranchisement… For many years she was also engaged in educational and philanthropic work in Birmingham. She was one of a number of women social reformers who for years delivered free lectures on hygiene and sanitation in the poorer parts of the city.'[243] The *Banbury Guardian* also included an obituary (Osler's daughter was married to a local doctor): 'She will, perhaps, be chiefly remembered as a protagonist of the Women's Suffrage Movement. She lived fortunately to see her aspirations acknowledged by the nation and the franchise extended to women, but it should be remembered that she was fighting the battle of political equality for her sex long before the rapid conversion of the community which was one of the effects of the late war. She steadfastly espoused the cause during the long years in which the movement was either bitterly opposed or treated with amused tolerance.' The progress of women's suffrage 'was due to a very large extent to the dauntless spirit which was displayed by a comparatively small but influential band of Birmingham women, of which Mrs Osler and her mother must be accounted the foremost, and to whose sane and inspiring leadership a great deal of the force of the movement was due'.[244]

In 1928, four years after Catherine Osler died, women were finally given the vote on equal terms with men. In that same year two opponents in the fight for female enfranchisement, former Prime Minster Herbert Henry Asquith and WSPU founder and leader Emmeline Pankhurst, both died; Millicent Fawcett died the year after. The battle for enfranchisement that so many women had fought was over. Now, finally, all men and women over the age of 21 could vote in general elections.

Afterword

In 1975, almost 60 years after some women were given the right to vote, Maude Smith, a dedicated suffragette, was interviewed at her home in Erdington. Maude was one of the last surviving WSPU members. Joining the organisation as a young woman, she had been driven to extreme militant behaviour by the lack of progress in securing women the right to vote, and by the frustration she felt at the failure of Government to respond to their arguments. Later, she became a victim of the brutal treatment meted out to hunger-striking women while in prison. In the interview Maude reminds us 'as long as you have a vote you must use it, and use it carefully'. Forty years on this statement is as important as ever: in 2018 there were only 208 female MPs, an overall total of 32%; the Fawcett Society (the name given in 1953 to the London Society for Women's Suffrage) continues to campaign for gender equality and women's rights, including the gender pay gap, which, according to current estimates by the Fawcett Society, will take 62 years to close; and, in 2015, a new political party, the Women's Equality Party, was formed specifically to campaign for gender equality to benefit all. Despite the sacrifices that many women made during the suffrage campaign, voter apathy has also been a serious problem in recent times, although there may be signs of change: in the UK 2017 General Election some 64% of voters aged 18-24 were thought to have voted, an increase on previous elections.

Although Birmingham women like Maude who were active participants in the campaign are not familiar names and many of the incidents that took place in the city have been forgotten, the Birmingham contribution to the cause had an important impact on the national story. The establishment of the, albeit short-lived, Female Political Union in the 1830s tells us that the city was ripe for reform and able to effectively mobilise and organise its citizens. Later on, Edgbaston in particular became an essential part of the story, giving rise to a network of mainly liberal social and civic campaigners like Eliza Sturge and Caroline Taylor, well-placed to set up the Birmingham Women's Suffrage Society that would work towards female suffrage and would focus its energies on constitutional and educational campaigning. Catherine Osler was an extremely important and influential player: her parents were founding members of the Birmingham Women's Suffrage Society and she was a subscriber from the age of 14, going on later to become President of the Society, a position she held for 20 years until her death in 1924. Her constant dedication, patience and commitment to the cause and to improving the lives of women were tireless.

As in the rest of the country, frustration with the slow progress that was being made in the late 19th century resulted in the rise of the WSPU. The active local branch in the city was led by a succession of passionate and enthusiastic young women such as Gladice Keevil, Dorothy Evans and Lilias Mitchell, who came to Birmingham to help encourage and galvanise the campaign. The local WSPU branch provided a home for the planning and execution of all sorts of militant activity – an attempted canal explosion, library arson, church vandalism and the slashing of a painting, to name but a few of the more serious incidents that took place. WSPU members like Maude Smith, along with Bertha Ryland and Hilda Burkitt, became embroiled in serious militant behaviour, including vandalism, arson, and bombings, behaviour certainly unexpected of women of the period, but these young and intelligent women wanted an equal say with men over how their lives would be lived, and wanted to help improve the lives of others. Their actions did not come without consequences, however, and all three women suffered greatly, both physically and mentally.

After the outbreak of war in the summer of 1914, Birmingham remained a suffrage stronghold, although direct campaigning ceased after the WSPU disbanded, and the BWSS focused on the war effort but they, along with the United Suffragists, were able to force politicians into recognising the contribution women had made, and the 'khaki' election of December 1918 saw three women – including Christabel Pankhurst (former WSPU leader) – run for West Midland seats. There may yet be more stories to emerge, new archives to be found, that will further elaborate on the strength and daring of these women campaigners.

The efforts that these women made, the time and dedication they gave, the impact on their health, the danger they put themselves in, and the treatment they suffered, should never be forgotten. They each recognised the power of the vote: in influencing Government policies that directly affected them; in having a say in how women's lives were lived; in participating in the democratic process. Although they had much to celebrate in 1918 and, later in 1928, they knew how much work would still have to be done. In 2018 we find ourselves in a position where full equality with men has yet to be achieved but we must take encouragement from the dedication of our suffrage sisters and continue to fight shoulder to shoulder.

Notes

1   West Midlands Police Museum, Police Orders, 18 September 1909; the term 'suffragette' was first used by the *Daily Mail* to describe members of the WSPU.

2   *Birmingham Daily Post*, 18 September 1909.

3   *The Common Cause*, 23 September 1909.

4   The Union had been established in 1829 in order to push for reform and the extension of the franchise to working-class men.

5   *Votes for Women*, 18 March 1910 .

6   Reekes, Andrew, *Speeches That Changed Britain* (West Midlands History Limited, Alcester, 2015), p. 23.

7   *The Birmingham Journal*, 18 August 1838.

8   *The Birmingham Journal*, 18 August 1838.

9   *The Birmingham Journal*, 25 August 1838.

10 Rogers, Helen, *Women and the People: Authority, Authorship and the Radical Tradition in Nineteenth-Century England* (Aldershot, 2000), p. 86.

11 *The Birmingham Journal*, 23 March 1839.

12 Rogers, H., *op. cit.*, p. 98.

13 Rogers, H., *op. cit*, p. 99.

14 'Votes for Women, the 1866 petition' [https://www.parliament.uk/business/committees/committees-a-z/commons-select/petitions-committee/petition-of-the-month/votes-for-women-the-1866-suffrage-petition/, accessed 20 April 2017].

15 Crawford, Elizabeth, 'From Frederick Street to Winson Green: the women's suffrage movement in Birmingham 1866-1918' (London, 2008), p. 1. Crawford suggests that the women were probably asked by friends or relations from outside the area to add their names.

16 Crawford, E., *op. cit.*, p. 2.

17 The Birmingham Ladies Negro's Friends Society for the Relief of Negro Slaves was established in 1825 by Lucy Townsend and Mary Lloyd.

18 July 1868, p. 529.

19 Bartley, Paula, 'Moral Regeneration: Women and the Civic Gospel in Birmingham, 1870-1914', *Midlands History* (2000, 25:1), p. 144.

20 Birmingham Women's Suffrage Society Reports, 1868-69.

21 16 May 1868.

22 October 1868, p. 73.

23 *Birmingham Daily Post*, 6 December 1871

24 Crawford, E., *op. cit.*, p. 4.

25 *Birmingham Daily Post*, 23 January 1874.

26 *Birmingham Daily Post*, 23 January 1874.

27 *Birmingham Daily Post*, 18 April 1877.

28 Mason was MP for Ashton-under-Lyne.

29 *Birmingham Daily Post*, 27 January 1883.

30 Woodall was Liberal MP for Stoke-upon-Trent.

31 BWSS Report, 1885.

32 This is most likely a reference to John Bright, MP for Birmingham Central, who had presented the petition to Parliament on behalf of the Society in 1868; BWSS Report, 1888.

33 Crawford, E., *op. cit.*, p. 8.

34 *Birmingham Daily Post*, 21 April 1890.

35 'An Appeal Against Women's Suffrage'. *The Nineteenth Century*, June 1889 [https://www.nationalarchives.gov.uk/education/britain1906to1918/transcript/g3cs2s1t.htm, accessed 7 December 2017] It is not known if any of the women were from Birmingham.

36 BWSS Report, 1892.

37 *South Wales Daily News*, 17 October 1896.

38 BWSS Report, 1898.

39 Crawford, E., *op. cit.*, p. 10.

40 Crawford, E., *op. cit.*, p. 8; Bartley, P., *op. cit.*, p. 145.

41 Reekes, Andrew, *The Birmingham Political Machine* (West Midlands History Limited, Alcester, 2018), p. 12.

42 Holton, Sandra Stanley, 'National Union of Women's Suffrage Societies (*act.* 1896–1918)', *Oxford Dictionary of National Biography*, Oxford University Press [http://www.oxforddnb.com/view/theme/96378, accessed 20 April 2017].

43 Cradley Heath in the Black Country had been a centre of nail and chain making from the early 19th century.

44 BWSS Report, 1903-4.

45 Holton, *op. cit., DNB*.

46 Barnsby, George, *Birmingham Working People: A History of the Labour Movement in Birmingham 1650-1914* (Wolverhampton, 1989), p. 197, p. 465.

47 Cadbury, E., Matheson, C. E., Shann, G., *Women's Work and Wages, A Phase of Life in an Industrial City* (London, 1907).

48 Barnsby, G., *op. cit.*, p. 466.

49 2 June 1906.

50 'Topics of the Day', *The Spectator*, 16 March 1907 [http://archive.spectator.co.uk/article/16th-march-1907/4/topics-of-the-day, accessed 20 April 2017].

51 'News of the Week', *The Spectator*, 16 March 1907 [http://archive.spectator.co.uk/page/16th-march-1907/1, accessed 20 April 2017].

52 'Topics of the Day', *The Spectator*, 16 March 1907 [http://archive.spectator.co.uk/article/16th-march-1907/4/topics-of-the-day, accessed 20 April 2017].

53 'Female Suffrage', *The Spectator*, 23 March 1907 [http://archive.spectator.co.uk/article/23rd-march-1907/14/female-suffrage, accessed 20 April 2017].

54 Crawford, E., *op. cit.*, p. 10.

55 Frederick Lawrence, a barrister, and Emmeline Pethick, an active socialist and campaigner, took each other's surnames when they married in 1901. Frederick was the only male member of the WSPU until he and Emmeline were expelled from the organisation in 1912.

56 Cowman, Krista, *Women of the Right Spirit: Paid Organisers of the Women's Social and Political Union 1904-1918* (Manchester University Press, Manchester, 2007), p. 46.

57 Nell Kenney was the sister of Annie Kenney, who had been arrested, along with Christabel Pankhurst, in Manchester in 1905. Prior to arriving in the Midlands, Nell had been working for the WSPU in the North-East.

58 *Votes for Women*, November 1907

59 BWSS Report 1906-7.

60 Speech delivered by Sir Oliver Lodge at the annual meeting of the Birmingham & Midlands Women's Suffrage Society, 28 May 1902, University of Birmingham Cadbury Research Library, UC9/v/3.

61 *Votes for Women*, 12 December 1907.

62 *Yorkshire Post*, 6 December 1907.

63 *The Mermaid*, February 1908.

64 *Votes for Women*, 5 March 1908.
65 *Votes for Women*, 26 March 1908.
66 Crawford, E., *The Women's Suffrage Movement: A Reference Guide 1866-1928* (London, 1999), p. 313.
67 *Votes for Women*, 23 July 1908.
68 From 1908 the WSPU had adopted these colours: green symbolised hope, white stood for purity and purple represented dignity.
69 *Votes for Women*, 26 November 1908.
70 *Bournville Works Magazine*, 1907.
71 *Bournville Works Magazine,* November 1908.
72 *Votes for Women*, 24 December 1908.
73 *The Common Cause*, 13 May 1909.
74 *The Common Cause*, 17 June 1909.
75 *Votes for Women*, 14 May 1909.
76 *The Common Cause*, 7 June 1909.
77 *Votes for Women*, 5 March 1909.
78 *Votes for Women*, 19 March 1909.
79 *Votes for Women*, 19 March 1909.
80 *Votes for Women*, 14 May 1909.
81 *Votes for Women*, 11 June 1909.
82 *Votes for Women*, 2 July 1909.
83 *Votes for Women*, 16 July 1909.
84 *Votes for Women*, 23 July 1909.
85 West Midlands Police Museum, Police Orders, 18 September 1909.
86 *Votes for Women*, 24 September 1909.
87 *Birmingham Daily Post*, 18 September 1909.
88 *Votes for Women*, 24 September 1909.
89 Ellen Barnwell was born in Birmingham in 1881 and was married in 1908 to a school attendance officer. The anti-Asquith protest appears to have been her only experience of militancy [http://www.uncoveryourancestors.org/blog/previous/2, accessed 8 September 2017].
90 *Birmingham Weekly Mercury*, 18 January 1908.
91 *London Daily News*, 2 April 1909; *Leeds Mercury,* 11 August 1909.
92 *The Common Cause*, 23 September 1909.
93 *The Common Cause*, 30 September 1909.
94 Austen Chamberlain, son of Joseph, was MP for East Worcestershire and had been Chancellor of the Exchequer until 1906 but was now in opposition to the Government. Like Asquith, he was a staunch anti-suffragist and had consistently voted against women's suffrage.
95 Grant, K., 'British Suffragettes and the Russian Method of Hunger Strike', *Comparative Studies in Society and History* (Vol. 53, No. 1, January 2011), p. 114.
96 Home Office: Registered Papers, Supplementary, HO 45/10418/183577, National Archives.
97 Home Office: Registered Papers, Supplementary, HO 45/10418/183577, National Archives.
98 Miller, I., 'A Prostitution of the Profession? Forcible Feeding, Prison Doctors, Suffrage and the British State, 1909-1914', *Social History of Medicine* (Vol. 26, Issue 2, May 2013), p. 10.
99 Labour MP for Blackburn and husband of Ethel Snowden, who had participated in the BWSS 'Indignation meeting'.
100 Liberal MP for West Ham North.
101 1 October 1909.

[102] Library of Birmingham, Minutes of Winson Green Visiting Committee, PS/B/4/5/1/3.

[103] *Votes for Women*, 1 October 1909.

[104] *Votes for Women*, 12 November 1909; *The Times*, 5 November 1909.

[105] *Votes for Women*, 26 November 1909.

[106] *Votes for Women*, 22 October 1909; *Daily News*, 18 October 1909.

[107] Home Office: Registered Papers, Supplementary, HO 45/10418/183577, National Archives.

[108] Holton, Sandra Stanley, *Suffrage Days: Stories from the Women's Suffrage Movement* (London, 1996), p. 125.

[109] *Votes for Women*, 24 December 1909.

[110] BWSS Report, 1908-9.

[111] BWSS Report, 1909-10.

[112] BWSS Report, 1909-10.

[113] Catherine Osler's, son, Julian, was a member of the Men's League for Women's Suffrage.

[114] *The Common Cause*, 6 January 1910.

[115] *The Common Cause*, 13 January 1910.

[116] BWSS Report, 1909-10.

[117] *The Common Cause*, 20 January 1910.

[118] BWSS Report, 1909-10.

[119] BWSS Report, 1909-10.

[120] *The Common Cause*, 21 July 1910.

[121] *Votes for Women*, 15 July 1910.

[122] *The Common Cause*, 17 November 1910.

[123] Crawford, E., *op. cit.*, p. 15.

[124] *Votes for Women*, 4 February 1910.

[125] *The Common Cause*, 1 December 1910.

[126] *Votes for Women*, 14 October 1910.

[127] *Votes for Women*, 11 November 1910.

[128] *Votes for Women*, 18 November 1910.

[129] Crawford, E., *op. cit.*, p. 16.

[130] *Votes for Women*, 25 November 1910.

[131] *Votes for Women*, 25 November 1910.

[132] Crawford, E., *op. cit.*, p. 17.

[133] Oral Evidence on the Suffragettes and Suffragist Movements: the Brian Harrison Interviews, Maude Kate Smith, 14 January 1975, Women's Library, LSE.

[134] *Votes for Women*, 16 December 1910.

[135] *Votes for Women*, 31 March 1911.

[136] 31 March 1911.

[137] Liddington, Jill, *Vanishing for the Vote: Suffrage, Citizenship and the Battle for the Census* (Manchester, 2014), pp. 337-341.

[138] *Votes for Women*, 7 April 1911.

[139] 'Crawford, E., 'Suffrage Stories: An Entire Birmingham College Boycotts the 1911 Census', [https://womanandhersphere.com/tag/anstey-college/, accessed 15 December 2017].

[140] In *Vanishing for the Vote* Liddington and Crawford give the number of census evaders in England as 572, p. 4.

[141] BWSS Report, 1911.

[142] *Votes for Women*, 5 January 1912.

143 Pankhurst, Christabel, 'Broken Windows', p. 5 in Mulvey Roberts, Marie & Mizuta, Tamae, eds., *Perspectives on the History of British Feminism. The Militants: Suffragette Activism* (London & Tokyo, 1994).

144 'I was raised by a secret suffragette', *The Telegraph*, 21 November 2015, [http://www.telegraph.co.uk/women/life/my-step-mum-secret-suffragette/, accessed 29 October 2017].

145 *Votes for Women*, 29 March 1912.

146 *The Times*, 1 April 1912.

147 Home Office: Registered Papers, Supplementary, HO144/1205/221862, National Archives.

148 25 April 1912.

149 Oral Evidence on the Suffragettes and Suffragist Movements: the Brian Harrison Interviews, Maude Kate Smith, 14 January 1975, Women's Library, LSE.

150 Home Office: Registered Papers, Supplementary, HO 45/10418/183577, National Archives.

151 *Votes for Women*, 5 July 1912.

152 *Votes for Women*, 1 November 1912.

153 *The Suffragette* magazine had been set up in 1912 by Christabel Pankhurst after the Pethick Lawrences, editors of *Votes for Women*, had been expelled from the WSPU. The first edition of *The Suffragette* was published on 18 October 1912; 12 December 1912.

154 Holton, *op. cit.*, p. 187.

155 Holton, *op. cit.*, pp. 176-177.

156 Crawford, E., *op. cit.*, p. 19.

157 BWSS Report, 1912-13.

158 British Library, 'Learning: Dreamers and Dissenters, NUWSS', [http://www.bl.uk/learning/histcitizen/21cc/struggle/suffrage/sources/source8/nuwss.html, accessed 15 December 2017].

159 *Staffordshire Advertiser*, 2 August 1914.

160 Holton, Sandra Stanley, *Feminism and Democracy: Women's Suffrage and Reform Politics in Britain 1900-1918* (Cambridge, 1986), p. 117.

161 BWSS Report, 1913-14.

162 Shoebridge, Michelle, 'The Women's Suffrage Movement in Birmingham and District 1903-1919', (unpublished MA thesis, 1983), p. 44-45.

163 Crawford, E. *op. cit.*, p. 19.

164 21 February 1913.

165 'Mrs Pankhurst's Maenads', *The Times*, 22 March 1912.

166 Leneman, Leah, *A Guid Cause: The Woman's Suffrage Movement in Scotland* (Edinburgh, 1995), p. 73.

167 Oral Evidence on the Suffragettes and Suffragist Movements: the Brian Harrison Interviews, Maude Kate Smith, 14 January 1975, Women's Library, LSE.

168 *The Suffragette*, 25 July 1913.

169 Crawford. E., *op cit*, Reference Guide, p. 259.

170 Mary Richardson claimed to have been present when Emily Davison jumped out in front of the King's horse at the Epsom Derby in June 1913. She campaigned alongside Sylvia Pankhurst, sister of Christabel, in East London, and both had been arrested in July after a rally.

171 *The Suffragette*, 24 October 1913.

172 31 October 1913.

173 *The Suffragette*, 14 November 1913.

174 *Votes for Women*, 17 October 1913.

175 *The Times*, 13 February 1914.

176 *The Common Cause*, 27 March 1914.

177 16 March 1914.

178 *Birmingham Daily Post*, 16 March 1914.

179 Library of Birmingham, St Philip's Cathedral, Minute Book, 23 April 1914.

180 Letter from Percy Adams, 14 Vernon Road, Edgbaston, 19 March 1914.

181 This is Sara Margery Fry (1874-1958), at that time Warden of the Hall of Residence for women students at the University of Birmingham.

182 *Birmingham Daily Mail*, 19 March 1914

183 *Birmingham Daily Post*, 16 May 1914.

184 *Birmingham Daily Mail*, 18 May 1914.

185 *The Suffragette*, 22 May 1914.

186 Library of Birmingham, Museum & Gallery Committee Minutes, BCC/1/BQ/1/1/1, 10 June 1914, p. 113.

187 'Exhibit A', Home Office: Registered Papers, Supplementary. HO 144/1205/221862, National Archives.

188 *Birmingham Mail*, 16 June 1914.

189 Library of Birmingham, Museum & Gallery Committee Minutes, BCC/1/BQ/1/1/1, 20 April 1914, p. 101.

190 Oral Evidence on the Suffragettes and Suffragist Movements: the Brian Harrison Interviews, Maude Kate Smith, 14 January 1975, Women's Library, LSE.

191 *Birmingham Daily Post*, 16 June 1914.

192 *Birmingham Gazette*, 15 June 1914.

193 *The Suffragette*, 10 July 1914.

194 Letter, 25 September 1914, Home Office: Registered Papers, Supplementary. HO 144/1205/221862, National Archives.

195 Library of Birmingham, Museum & Gallery Committee Minutes, BCC/1/BQ/1/1/1, 16 November 1914, p. 135.

196 Library of Birmingham, Museum & Gallery Committee Minutes, BCC/1/BQ/1/1/1, 19 April 1915, p. 159.

197 Smith, Angela K., *Suffrage Discourse in Britain during the First World War* (Farnham, 2005), p. 1.

198 7 August 1914.

199 *The Common Cause*, 28 August 1914.

200 Vellacott, Jo, *Pacifists, Patriots and the Vote: the Erosion of Democratic Suffragism in Britain during the First World War* (Basingstoke, 2007), p. 17.

201 BWSS Report, 1914-15.

202 BWSS Report, 1914-15.

203 Purvis, June, 'Emmeline Pankhurst in the Aftermath of Suffrage, 1918-1928' in Gottlieb, Julie & Toye, Richard, (eds.), *The Aftermath of Suffrage: Women, Gender, and Politics in Britain, 1918-1945* (Basingstoke, 2013), p. 19.

204 Vellacott, J., *op. cit.*, p. 20.

205 Petition, 7 August 1914, Home Office: Registered Papers, Supplementary. HO 144/1205/222030, National Archives.

206 Holloway Prison Daily Report, 8 August 1914, Home Office: Registered Papers, Supplementary. HO 144/1205/222030, National Archives.

207 Crawford. E., *op. cit.*, Reference Guide, p. 259.

208 Birmingham Museum & Art Gallery, Collection of papers relating to Nellie Hall.

209 7 August 1914.

210 *Votes for Women*, 26 March 1915.

211 *Votes for Women*, 19 February 1915.

212 *Votes for Women*, 12 March 1915. Dorothy Evans helped establish the Independent WSPU in March 1916.

213 Oral Evidence on the Suffragettes and Suffragist Movements: the Brian Harrison Interviews, Maude Kate Smith, 14 January 1975, Women's Library, LSE.

214 Roberts, Sian, *Birmingham, Remembering 1914-18* (Stroud, 2014), p. 107.

215 Gullace, Nicoletta F., 'Christabel Pankhurst and the Smethwick Election: right-wing feminism, the Great War and the ideology of consumption', *Women's History Review*, 23:3 (2014), p. 332.

216 *Votes for Women*, 17 December 1915.

217 Vellacott, J., *op. cit.*, p. 61.

218 Vellacott, J., *op. cit.*, p. 92.

219 Wiltsher, Anne, *Most Dangerous Women* (London, 1985), p. 80.

220 *Staffordshire Advertiser*, 12 August 1916.

221 Gullace, N. F., *op. cit.*, p. 332.

222 BWSS Report, 1916-17.

223 BWSS Report, 1916-17.

224 BWSS Report, 1916-17.

225 30 June 1917 .

226 *Votes for Women*, February 1918.

227 The NUWSS became the National Union of Societies for Equal Citizenship.

228 Osler, Catherine, 'At Last!', *Women Workers, Quarterly Magazine of the Birmingham Branch of the National Union of Women Workers*, March 1918, pp. 95-99.

229 Purvis, June, 'The Women's Party of Great Britain (1917-1919): a forgotten episode in British women's political history', *Women's History Review* (2016), p. 640.

230 Gullace, N. F., *op. cit.*, p. 333.

231 *Birmingham Daily Post*, 11 February 1918.

232 Smith, Angela K., 'The Pankhursts and the War: Suffrage magazines and First World War propaganda', *Women's History Review* (2006), p. 109.

233 Purvis, J., *op. cit.*, *Aftermath*, pp. 20-21. The Parliament (Qualification of Women) Act was passed on 21 November 1918.

234 Purvis, J., *op. cit.*, 'Women's Party', p. 641.

235 Gullace, N. F., *op. cit.*, p. 333.

236 Purvis, J., *op. cit.*, 'Women's Party', p. 645.

237 Gullace, N. F., *op. cit.*, pp. 338-340.

238 John, Angela V., 'Mary Reid Macarthur', *Oxford Dictionary of National Biography*, Oxford University Press [http://www.oxforddnb.com.ezproxye.bham.ac.uk/view/article/30411, viewed 22 December 2017].

239 BWSS Report, 1918-1919.

240 BWSS Report, 1918-1919.

241 Crawford, E., *op. cit.*, Reference Guide, p. 481.

242 BWSS Report, 1919-1920.

243 18 December 1924.

244 25 December 1924.

Index

Note: italics indicate images; 'n' indicates end notes.

advertising *see* publicity and propaganda

age restrictions 101–2

Aldis, Mrs 26

Alum Rock Road 51, 56

Anglican Church 84–5; *see also* Birmingham
    Cathedral

Anstey, Rhoda 60–1

Anstey Physical Training College 60–1, 98

anti-suffragist movement 1, 16–17, *32, 33*, 37–8,
    45, 50, 60; 'Mysterious Fifty' group *71*, 87–8

'Appeal Against Female Suffrage' 16–17

arrests 1, 26–7, 39–40, 42, 43, 58, 62, 65, 79–80, 90;
    see also imprisonment; police; trials

arson 65, *70*, 78, 79–83, 86–7, 90, 92

artwork vandalism *72, 73*, 88–91, 95

Ash, Mrs 7

Ashby, Margery Corbett *75*

Ashford, Mrs 14, 18

Asquith, Herbert Henry 1, 25–7, *29*, 40–4, 51–7,
    62, 67, 76, 79–80, 92, 100, 107

Aston 24, 27, 56

Aston Manor Parliament *29*, 42–3

'At-Home' meetings 24, 27, 36, 39, 98

Attwood, Thomas 5

Balmoral, golf course incident 78

Banbury Guardian, The 106

Barnwell, Ellen 1, 42, 46, 112n89

Becker, Lydia 7

Berkswell 37–8

Bills to Parliament on women's suffrage 9, 12,
    14, 22; Conciliation Bill (1910) 54, 57, 61–3,
    85; private members' 18, 20, 22, 23, 62

Bingley Hall demonstration (1909) 1–3, *29*, 41–5, 51

Birmingham Cathedral, vandalism 83–6

Birmingham Daily Gazette, The 52, *71*, 87, 99, 106

Birmingham Daily Mail, The 63, 67, 82–3, 85

Birmingham Daily Post, The 9, 12, 16, 81–5, 91, 102

Birmingham Journal, The 5, 8, 9

Birmingham Ladies Union of Workers 19

Birmingham Lady Mayoress's depot 95

Birmingham Men's Political Union for Women's
    Enfranchisement 56

Birmingham Museum and Art Gallery, vandalism 4,
    72, 88–9, 91

Birmingham Owl, The 41

Birmingham Pictorial & Dart, The 34, 46–7, 49,
    54–5, 60

Birmingham Political Union (BPU) 5, 6

Birmingham School Board 11, 12

Birmingham Society for Equal Citizenship 103

Birmingham Weekly Mercury, The 42–3

Birmingham Weekly Newspaper, The 38

Birmingham Women's Liberal Association 1, 13,
    15, 49

Birmingham Women's Social & Political Union
    27, 36, 38–9, 50, 57, 77, 79, 89–90, 96, 98

Birmingham Women's Suffrage Society (BWSS)
    1–4, 7–10, 12–19, 21–5, *33*, 44, 51–7, 67, 76, 85–
    6, 95, 101, 103, 108; annual reports 3, 14, 17, 19,
    37, 51, 53, 62, 66, 93, 106

'Black Friday' 57–8, 65

Blakeman Welsh, Mr *30*

Bloxham, Mr *30*

bombings 78–9, 81

Bordesley 52

Bournville 36

Bournville Works Magazine 36

Brewster, Bertha 27, 97–8, 100

Bridge Street 45

Bright, Jacob 9, 12

Bright, John 8–9, 11, 110n32

Bristol Road 61

Broad Street 10

Broad Street Corner 12

Budget League Demonstration 1

Bull Ring 38, 47, 52, 55, 56, 90, 98

Burkitt, Hilda 1, 4, *30*, 37, 39, 42–3, 46–50, 56–62,
    64, 81, 90, 95–6

Cadbury, Mrs George 18

Cadbury, Sir Edward 19, 36, 85

Cadbury's factory 36

Cambridge Street 1, 42

Camp Hill 39

Campbell-Bannerman, Henry 21–2, 25
Cannon Hill Park 40, 87
canvassing 37, 56
Cassels, Dr William 46, 47
Cecil, Lord 100
census boycotts *34*, 59–61
Central National Society for Women's Suffrage 16, 17
Chad Road, Edgbaston 7
chalking pavements *31*, 48, 57, 60
Chamberlain, Austen 18, 45, 53, 112n94
Chamberlain, Beatrice 53
Chamberlain, Clara 13
Chamberlain, Joseph 13, 14, 18, 53
Chartist movement 5–6, 11
Church League for Women's Suffrage 84–5
Church of the Messiah, Broad Street 10
churches, targeting of 80, 83–5
Clark, Sarah 7
Clarke, Alice M. 60
class, social 2, 18–20, 22, 56; *see also* middle-class women; working-class women
Classical Association 27
Clausen, George, *Primavera* 89–90, 95
Collings, Jesse 18
Colmore Row 24, 63
Common Cause, The (NUWSS newspaper) 2, 3, *32*, 37, 43–5, 48–9, 51, 53–5, 57, 82, 93
Conciliation Bill (1910) 54, 57, 61–3, 85; 'Black Friday' 57–8, 65
Conservative Party 14–15, 22, 59
constitutional suffrage 6, 21–2, 24, 38, 40, 44, 45, 52, 66
Cooper, Selina 44
Corbett Ashby, Margery 105
Corporation Street 90
Cotteridge Public Hall 86
Courier, The 88
Cradley Heath 19, *35*, 56, 58, 76, 111n43
Crawford, Elizabeth 3, 16, 18, 60, 110n15
cross-dressing 1, 42
Crosskey, Reverend 10, 12, 13, 16–18
Cunard, Ida 26

Daily Telegraph, The 97–8
Davis, May 39
Davison, Emily Wilding 88, 114n170
Dawson, George 10
deputations to Parliament 18, 21, 26–7, 36, 39, 40, 44, 53, 62
Dixon, George 10, 11, 14, 18
Dorridge 85

Easy Row 37, 45, 61, 67
Edgbaston 7, 13, 18, *34*, 57, 59, 60, *69*, 85, 87, 90, 98, 108
Edgbaston Assembly Rooms 27
Edgbaston Road 40
Edmonds, George 5–6
Education Act (1870) 11
Edwards, Marie 26, 39
Englishwoman's Review 8, 9
equality 10, 96–7, 104, 108
Erdington 60–1, 108
Estcourt, Constance 60
Estcourt, Doris 60
Ethel Street 27
Evans, A. W. 38
Evans, Dorothy 55–9, 62, 98, 109
Evans, Harold 79
Evening Despatch, The 52
Exchange Assembly Rooms 7

factories 24, 36, 38, 39, 40–1, 111n43
'Fallowfield', Norfolk Road 13
Fawcett, Millicent Garrett 2–3, 9–10, 13, 16, 17, *28*, 67, 99–101, 107
Fawcett Society 108
Female Political Union 5–6, 20, 108
forcible feeding *31, 32*, 45–50, 63–4, *68*, 83–4, 90–1, 95–6
Francis Road 57
Friends of Women's Suffrage 76, 93
Fry, Sarah Margery 86, 115n181

Gardner, Miss 53
Gawthorpe, Mary 23

General Elections (1910) 51–3, 55, 57, 59
General Election ('khaki' election) (1918) *75*, 103–7, 109
George Road 60
girls 38–9
Gladstone, William 14, 16
Globe, The 29
golf course vandalism 78
Gooch Street 52
Gore-Booth, Eva 19, 44
Great King Street 67
Great Reform Act (1832) 5
Griffiths, Miss 85
Griffiths-Boscawen, Major 59

Hagley Road 58, 60
Hall, Leonard 58
Hall, Nellie (Emmeline) 47, 58, 79–80, 96, 102
Hall, Pattie 58, 60
Haly, Margaret 90, 98
Handsworth 46, 56, 58; boathouse arson *70, 78*
Harborne 87
Harborne Road 85
Hardie, Keir 20, 46
Harold Road *34*, 60
Hazel, Gladys 27, *34*, 37, 47, 57, 59, 60, 62
Helby, Dr 46
Hemming, Laura 26
Hermitage Road 13, 59, *69*, 87, 98
Hill, J. Ernest 91
Hill, Sylvia 39
Hockley 67
Holloway Prison 26, 39, 62, 64, 84, 95
Holly Road 56
Home Office 45–6, 48, 58, 64, 91, 95
Home Rule for Ireland 16
Hood, Susannah 7
Hooper, A. G. 59
householders 54, 56, 61, 102
hunger strikes 3, 43, 45, 63, *68*, 77, 80, 87, 89–90; forcible feeding *31, 32*, 45–50, 63–4, *68*, 83–4, 90–1, 95–6

imprisonment 26–7, *31, 32*, 36, 38, 39, 43, 45, 58, 63, 90–1, 97–8
Independent Labour Party (ILP) 20, 36, 58
International Suffrage Alliance 93

Jeffs, Waller 48
John Bright Street 57, 58, 79, 87
Johnson, Mary 7, 9
Jones, Helena 27

Keevil, Gladice 27, *30*, 38–40, 50, 55, 109
Kenney, Annie 20
Kenney, Nell 24, *30*, 111n57
Kent Street 60
Kerwood, Edith 26–7, 77
King Edward's Girls Grammar School 27, 39, 59
King's Norton Educational Board 27
King's Norton train station attack *70*, 82–3
Kirby, Miss 52

Labour Exchange 90
Labour Party 20, 22, 46, 66, 76
Lancashire and Cheshire Textile and Other Workers Representation Committee 19
Lansbury, George 20
lanterns 57
Lapworth, Mrs 6
Leigh, Mary 1, 42, 46, 47
Liberal Party 14–15, 20–2, 40, 44, 49, 53, 55, 66
library arson 80–1
Liddington, Jill 60
Lloyd George, David 1, 51, 59, 81, 97, 100, 104
Lodge, Sir Oliver 25, 106
London Society for Women's Suffrage 7, 10, 108
Lowe, Sir Francis 55
Lozells 60

Macarthur, Mary *35*, 56, *75*, 105
McKenzie, Georgina 36
McLaren, Priscilla Bright 9
Manchester 2, 20
Manchester National Society for Women's Suffrage 7, 9, 19

manhood suffrage 2, 5, 7, 14, 17, 62

married women 8, 16, 20, 54–5, 60

Married Women's Property Act (1870) 8

Married Women's Property Act (1882) 13–14

Marsh, Charlotte 1, 42, 46–8

Martineau, Mrs 95

Mason, Hugh 13

Masonic Hall 9

Masterman, Mr 46

Matheson, Cecile 19

Men's League for Women's Suffrage 38

Men's Political Union 58, 79

Mercury, The 49–50

Mermaid, The (student newspaper) 25

middle-class women 2, 19, 22, 62–3, 77

Middlemore, John 10

Midland Institute 11

militancy 1–4, 6, 13, 20, 21–7, 36–50, 61–2, 64–7, *71*, 77–86; *see also* arrests; arson; bombings; vandalism; window-smashing

Mill, John Stuart 7–9, 12, 16

Mitchell, Lilias 78, 80, 86–7, 90, 95, 109

Mitchener, Leonard 96

Monument Road 38

Moseley Road 38, 52

munitions production *74*, 97

Muntz, Philip Henry 11

'Mysterious Fifty' anti-suffragists *71*, 87–8

National Federation of Women Workers 36, 56

National League for Opposing Women's Suffrage 53

National Society for Women's Suffrage 10, 11, 15–17

National Union of Women Workers 103

National Union of Women's Suffrage Societies (NUWSS) 2, 17–18, 21, 23, *35*, 48–9, 53, 55, 61, 66, 76, 93, 99, 101; Election Fighting Fund 66, 76; Pilgrimage (1913) 67, 76, 92; *see also Common Cause, The* (newspaper)

National Women's Anti-Suffrage League 53

New Street 7, 40, 60

Newdegate, Francis 63, *69*

Newman Hall, Reverend William Aidan 85

Nineteenth Century, The (magazine) 16–17

Norfolk Road 13

Northfield 39

Northfield Library (*earlier* Carnegie Library) 4, *70*, 80–1

Nursery Road 60

Olton Lawn Tennis Club 83

Oratory Cricket Club 87

Osler, Alfred 13, 16

Osler, Catherine Courtauld (*née* Taylor) 1–4, 12–19, 21, *28*, 44, 61–2, 66, 99, 101–3, 106–8; relations with the press 23, 49, 53–4, 81–2

pacifism 98–100, 104

Pankhurst, Christabel (daughter of Emmeline) 2, 3, 20, 24, 25, *28*, 51, 61–2, 65, *75*, 81, 94, 100, 103–7

Pankhurst, Emmeline 2, 3, 20, 23, 24, *28, 29*, 38–40, 43, 57, 58, 78, 80, 89, 96–7, 100, 103, 107

Pankhurst, Sylvia (daughter of Emmeline) 2, 3, 20, *28*

Paradise Street 56, 57

Parliament Act (1911) 55

Parliamentary Franchise (Women) Bill (1912) 62

Pethick Lawrence, Emmeline 23, 24, 38, 64–5, 96, 111n55

Pethick Lawrence, Frederick 23, 64–5, 96, 111n55

police 1, 38, 41, 45–7, 52, 87

politics, women's involvement in 5–7, 14–15, 22–3

press 3, 17, 22, 27, 41, 49, 53–4, 62–3, 79, 85

Prisoners (Temporary Discharge for Ill-Health) Act ('The Cat and Mouse Act') (1913) *68*, 77, 80, 83, 87, 90

property qualification 2, 4, 8–9, 13–14, 21, 25, 99, 102

protests 16, 20, 23, 27, *35*, 67, 97–8; *see also* census boycotts; Bingley Hall demonstration; deputations to Parliament; hunger strikes

publicity and propaganda 20, 37, 45, 47, 51, 55–8, 61, 67, 77, 83–5, 99, 102; chalking pavements *31*, 48, 57, 60

Quarry Bank 58

Queen's College 54, 86, 98

Index

Rafter, Chief Constable 46

Redfern, Elizabeth 26, *30*, 36

Reform Act (1867) 7, 10

Reform Act (1884) 14

Reid, Edith (*née* Taylor) 16, 18, 49

Representation of the People Act (1918), women's clause 100–2

Richardson, Mary 1114n170

Ring, Florence 57–8, 61

Robertson, Miss 8

Robinson, Mr *30*

Romney, George, *John Bensley Thornhill as a Boy* (*c.*1784–5), vandalism of 4, *72*, 88–9, 91

Roper, Esther 19

Royal Academy, artwork vandalism 73, 89–90, 95

Russell Road 40

Ryland, Alice (Mrs W. H.) 13, 39, 91, 98

Ryland, Bertha 13, 36–7, 47, 59, 60, 62–3, 65, 66, *69*, *72*, 87–91, 95

Ryland, Frederick 13

Ryland, Henry 63, *69*

Ryland, William Henry 13, 85

St Augustine's Road 13

St Martin's Church 78

St Philip's Church 78, 80

Sale, Mr 78–9

Salt, Thomas Clutton 5–6

Saltley 39, 51

Sandford, Venerable Archdeacon 8

Scotsman, The 95

Selly Oak 1, 24

Shann, George 19, 36

single women 8, 16, 55, 56

Small Heath 27, 39, 56

Smethwick *75*, 103–7

Smith, Isabel Maude Kate (Maude Smith) *30*, 57–8, 60, 62, 63, *73*, 79, 89–90, 95, 98, 108

Snowden, Ethel 43, 45

Snowden, Philip 20

Soho Road 46, 52

Solihull 83

Southall, Gertrude 49

Southall, Mrs 18

Sparkbrook 1, 37

Spectator, The 21, 22–3

Spronson, Emma *31*

Staffordshire Advertiser, The 67, 78–9, 100

Stechford 58

Steelhouse Lane 1

Stone, Benjamin 18

Stourbridge constituency 23, 105

strikes 35, 56

Sturge, Eliza 5, 9–13, 18, 108

Sturge, Mary (niece of Eliza) 44

Suffragette, The (WSPU publication) 3, 65, 77, 80–1, 83, 91, 94–6, 114n153

'suffragettes', use of term 1, 110n1

taxation 22, 25, 51, 54

Taylor, Caroline 7, 10–13, 108

Taylor, Catherine *see* Osler, Catherine Courtauld (*née* Taylor)

Taylor, Clementia 7

Taylor, Edith *see* Reid, Edith (*née* Taylor)

Taylor, Miss L. R. 44, 45, 52

Taylor, Peter Alfred 7

Taylor, William 7, 10, 12

telephone wire cutting 78

tennis pavilion attacks 83

Times, The 77, 105

Town Hall 5, 10–11, 13–14, 24–5, 27, 36, 38, 40, 57, 104

Train, Elizabeth 7

train station arson 82–3

trials 62–3, *73*, 87, 90, 95

Ulster militants 87, 90

United Suffragists 96–100, 102

University of Birmingham 25, 40, 44, 106; graduates, enfranchisement of 102; students, anti-suffragist 38, 60

vandalism 4, *72*, *73*, 78, 83–6, 88–91, 95; *see also* arson; window-smashing

Varley, Julia *29*, 36

Victoria Square 47

violence *see* militancy

Votes for Women (publication of WSPU; later of United Suffragists) 3, 5, 21, 23–7, 38–40, 43, 48, 56, 58–62, 63, 84, 96–7, 102–3

Wallace-Dunlop, Marion 45

Walsall 49–50

Ward, Mrs Humphrey 16–17

Wednesbury 23

welfare 19–20

West Bromwich 23

West Midlands constituency 105

Wheeler, Mr *30*

Wheeleys Road 7, 13

widows 8, 55, 61

Wilson, Harold 56, 58

window-smashing 62–3, *69*, 77, 79–80, 90, 97

Winson Green Gaol 1, *32*, 42, 45–8, 58, 63, 87, 90, 98

Wolverhampton 23

womanhood suffrage, full 100–2

'woman's sphere' concept 10, 12, 13, 16–17, 53

Women Workers (magazine) 19

Women's Co-operative Guild 76

Women's Equality Party 108

Women's Freedom League 25, 59

Women's International League 98

Women's Liberal Association 44, 49

Women's Liberal Federation 15–16

'Women's Parliament, The' deputation 26–7

Women's Party 103–4

Women's Peace Crusade 98

Women's Social & Political Union (WSPU) 1–2, 4, 20–7, 41–2, 55, 58, 62, 64, 76–9, 87, 94–6, 109; colours and badge *33*, 36, 112n68; *see also* Birmingham Women's Social & Political Union; *Suffragette, The* (publication); *Votes for Women* (publication)

Women's Work and Wages report (1904–7) 19–20, 56

Wood, Mrs 26

working-class women 19–20, 24, *29*, *35*, 36, 39, 47, 56–7, 76, 93

World War One 4, *73*, *74*, 91–107; women's war effort 97–9

Yardley 92

Yardley Wood, canal bank attack 78–9

Yeomans, Morris 36

Yoxall, Elsie 49